Memories and Reflections

An East Neuk Anthology

Nellie Watson

Memories and Reflections: An East Neuk Anthology
By Nellie Watson

ISBN 9781794147386

Edited by Joan Watson, Meg Humphries and Alison Humphries
All poems copyright © Alison Humphries
Foreword copyright © Harry D. Watson 2018
Additional content copyright © Alison Humphries 2019

First published 1993 by Joan Bett Watson, Churchdown, Gloucestershire.
This edition published 2019 by Alison Humphries, Elton, Gloucestershire.

Please direct any enquiries to the publisher via ali_humphries@outlook.com.

Front cover image: Steam drifter 'The Pride O Fife' KY 218, in the 1930s, with William Smith (Bruce), who was Nellie's uncle, nearest to the bow. The tall man standing at the back of the boat is Salter Watson with his wife Georgina 'Jean' Anderson. Salter's father John Watson (Salter) owned the boat. (Photograph from the private Watson / Kingscott family collection.)

Back cover image: 'Herring Lassies'. (Kindly shared from the private Watson / Anderson family collection.)

Nellie borrowing her husband's overalls and bike

About the Author

Nellie Watson was born in 1895 in Cellardyke, Anstruther, the daughter of a fisherman. She was educated at Cellardyke Public School.

Writing poems and the study of human nature has become a 'way of life' for Nellie – "pushin' a pen for the sheer love of it", as she puts it.

She writes as the mood takes her, sometimes in "Fife's ain tongue" and other times in English, inspiration coming from looking, listening and remembering.

The past becomes alive as Nellie takes us on a fascinating journey through childhood, adolescence onwards, giving a vivid, witty and utterly truthful account of past times, people and places.

Joan Watson, Editor, 1993 edition

NELLIE WATSON

Acknowledgements

Reading, typing and researching for the second edition of Auntie Nellie's Memories and Reflections have been very thought-provoking. Revelling in the language of my childhood and being "held fast" by her wit and wisdom have both evoked memories and laughter, minute by minute. I especially enjoyed transcribing my old recording of Nellie and Mary. It's been hard work but also a real treat!

This is a book of poetry – but it isn't just a poetry book. Lashings of "oor ain tongue", our social history and a great sense of identity are all here, linked by the reality of daily life in a close-knit fishing community. My late mother, Joan Kingscott (née Watson) did us a great service when in 1993 she first published a selection of Auntie Nellie's poems. By including (until now) unpublished poems and also some written by Nellie's cousin, Peter Smith (Poetry Peter) in this edition, the hope is that a wider range of subjects have been addressed. My cousin James Kingscott Corstorphine has generously given me permission to publish poems by Peter Smith and credit also goes to him for the photographs of the 2018 Sea Queen Ceremony.

As a child I knew the voices of those who lived in Cellardyke by the way they spoke and the words they used. We were, of course, related to almost everyone! Folk's doors, and their hearts, were open. "You'll get what you give" (goodness and kindness will be returned) was our family maxim, and the gentle folk of Cellardyke certainly lived by that. There was a lot of what we would today call "emotional intelligence". Always interested and caring, a raised eyebrow – or a knowing nod – was as near as we ever came to that frowned-upon word "gossip"!

Without giving it much thought, I could identify those "Fifers" hailing from further afield. Cousin Jimmy recently described some differences: "in St. Monans they speak very slowly, and in Pittenweem, barely a mile distant, they speak very fast!" Regarding the fishing villages having their own words, cousin Davie Corstorphine gave this example: "Dykers hae Cutsies, Anster hae Seagulls, Pittenweem hae Cutties and the Droaners (Simminins) hae Maws." All being fiercely proud and protective of their own, the expression "We'll feed oor ain fish guts tae oor ain sea maws" means "We'll look after our own affairs, thank you!"

My thanks go to many. When needing assistance, I was incredibly fortunate to be able to call on my four super-patient and knowledgeable Cellardyke cousins and the legacy of their late parents, Sonny and Shirley (née Kingscott) Corstorphine. I am very grateful to them all.

As luck would have it, I was also able to ask an expert, Harry D. Watson, academic, linguist and translator, who was head of The Dictionary of The Older Scottish Tongue (DOST), a major Scottish language dictionary project, until its completion in 2001. My late mother was a contributor to the project and Harry is my third cousin once removed. Harry has kindly written the two-part Foreword for this book and for that I give my heartfelt thanks.

My thanks must also go to Linda Fitzpatrick of the Scottish Fisheries Museum; to Judith Hewitt at The Devil's Porridge Museum; to Richard Weymss, musician, composer and historian; to Kevin Dunion OBE, academic, author and historian; and to May Brydie who shared her recollections of working at the factory with my Auntie Lizzie and Auntie Chrissie Smith. Thanks, too, to the many users of Facebook who connect so readily when I'm researching. I have been pleased to find many other Dyker "cousins" along the way.

My heartfelt thanks go to my husband Tim, who is

always supportive and kind, and to our editor daughter Meg, who readily gives her expertise and encouragement. Really, I couldn't have done this without you two.

Lang may yer lum reek!

Alison Humphries (née Kingscott)
Email: ali_humphries@outlook.com

Contents

List of Poems

* = new for this edition

Poems Previously Published

The Winter Herring (*The Observer*, 1949)

Pause and Think (*Galaxy of Verse*, 1960)

The Sunset (*The People's Friend*, 1973)

The Plodder (*Poetry Now*, 1991)

Think Again (*Poetry Now*, 1992)

The Exile's View of Scotland (*Arrival Press*, 1993)

Note: The above poems were published under the name N. Smith.

Foreword

1. The Poetry of Cellardyke

Helen "Nellie" Watson was born in 1895 into a Cellardyke where "braid Scots" was the everyday language of the people, and the fishing industry was still the mainstay of the local economy. Educated at the local school, and marrying a local man after WWI, she had plenty of exposure to the local version of Scots and although she was to move around Scotland with her marine engineer husband, most of their married life was spent in Fife. Consequently, the Scots she employed in her poems was not much "tainted" by outside influences, although, like Robert Burns himself – the model for so many village poets in lowland Scotland and Ulster – she was also perfectly capable of writing in flawless English if she felt the subject-matter required it.

In a poem penned in 1948, she explained what inspired

her first venture into poetry. Having bought a birthday card for a very young relative, she was appalled by the quality of the verses inside, and thought she could do better herself (see page 96). She was far from being the first "Dyker" to try her hand at versifying. There was a tradition in Cellardyke, as in many other rural locations, of commemorating local events, from the edifying to the tragic, in verse, and the emergence of local news-sheets and, after the abolition of the stamp duty in 1855, of newspapers in the modern sense, provided an outlet for such versification.

In the East Neuk, the Pittenweem Register ruled supreme before the East of Fife Record made its appearance, and in one issue in 1849 Cellardyke fisherman Michael Doig reflected gloomily on the transience of life, no doubt prompted by the regular cholera outbreaks which decimated the populations of the East Neuk fishing towns:

> *While wand'ring in auld Nature's field, –*
> *The heart with sorrow pressed;*
> *A pensive thought the reapers yield,*
> *As they do glean the harvest store.*
>
> *While they cut down the golden corn*
> *That yestermorn did sweetly wave,*

It teaches man he's here forlorn,
And should prepare him for the grave ...

and so on, for three more stanzas. Apart from "auld" in the first line, the poem is written in impeccable standard English, presumably because of the grave (no pun intended!) subject-matter. Scots was usually felt to be more suitable for humorous and facetious subject-matter, the classic model here being Anstruther poet William Tennant's 1812 "Anster Fair". (A Cellardyke Watson on his mother's side, Tennant was distantly related to both Nellie Watson and the present writer.)

In a fishing village, disasters at sea were all too common, and would often be commemorated in verse by a local bard. In 1890, for example, the loss of the Garland and her crew of Dykers inspired an eleven-stanza elegy by a young fisherman called John Dick:

Slowly the morning dawned upon
Our gallant little fleet.
As o'er the bounding sea they sped,
Each little craft complete.

The heavy sky showed silent signs,
Which some alone can know;

But brave are they who face the storm
As they would meet a foe …

Once again the language is English, for the subject-matter is solemn and the poet seems to feel that the use of his native Scots would be out of place. The whole poem, which shows some literary merit, has almost the feel of a hymn. There are no elegies of this nature among Nellie Watson's published poems, although several Cellardyke fishermen were lost at sea in her lifetime.

The best-known poet of Cellardyke in the twentieth century was undoubtedly "Poetry Peter" Smith, a distant relative of Nellie's, whose verses were mainly written for recital at local gatherings. Towards the end of his life they were printed in two collections, and a new anthology was published in the year 2000 (see Bibliography). Peter and Nellie often voice the same concerns, for example Peter Smith's "The Herrin'", written in 1937 when the herring fishing was at its height, is echoed by Nellie's "The Winter Herring", written in 1949 when that particular fishery was going through hard times. Both poets eulogise the stirring sight of the herring fleet setting out for the fishing grounds. Here is Peter Smith:

The shades o' nicht were drappin' fast,

When oot o' Anster Harbour passed
A fleet o' craft o' various sort,
A' keen to catch – but no' for sport,
The herrin'.

... The sicht was bonnie, without doot,
Tae see them as they a' sailed oot,
Alert and skilfu' was each man,
Eager the slightest sign tae scan –
O' herrin'.

But those happy days were long gone by the time Nellie wrote her poem:

I wonder what has happened tae
The HERRING in the Firth of Forth –
Long syne the boats cam sailin' there –
Frae ports faur sooth, and wast, and north.

A cheery pictur' they aye made
On bonny, clear and starry nichts,
When ower the watter there ye saw
The Firth filled wi' their twinklin' lichts.

Both poets intersperse their Scots words with standard English, obviously finding it hard to write one hundred per cent in Scots. Nellie's "long syne" is a bit of an English/Scots mishmash, where "lang syne" might have been expected, and she writes the Burnsian "frae" instead of the usual Cellardyke "fae". Otherwise, a line like "Frae ports faur sooth, and wast, and north" has an authentic Cellardyke ring to it.

Village poets will often insert into their poems some local colour, providing useful insights into how people lived and worked in the town. In Cellardyke, carters like "Ecky Steenson" (Alex. Stevenson) would transport nets from the harbour to the fishermen's houses, dumping them in front of the house for mending, usually by the women. In the case of East Forth Street, where Nellie's family lived, that meant dumping the nets in the "brick", the paved area between the house and the pavement:

> *The menfolk toiled for mony an oor',*
> *The womenfolk kept busy tae –*
> *For Ecky Steenson's horse and cairt –*
> *Gaed rumblin' thro' the streets each day.*
>
> *Wi plenty torn nets for a'*
> *Some screeded (torn) richt intae the core,*

He jist wid shout their names – and then
Dump doon the nets, richt at their door!

Nellie's poem "The Tattie Howkin'" is a heartfelt account of the backbreaking work of picking potatoes in the fields around Cellardyke, a seasonal occupation that provided some useful pin-money for, mainly, the women and older children of the area (including this writer in his schooldays). Written in 1950, the action of the poem takes place forty years earlier in 1910, when Nellie and her friend Alice picked potatoes at Caiplie Toll, to the east of Cellardyke.

A worset shawl was tied around
Oor breest – that was for need,
Anither ane was flung across
Oor shoothers and oor heid!

A packsheet apron tied across
Oor front and no jist aince,
'Twas tied baith at the waist and knees –
The like we've ne'er worn since!

...We worked gey hard at pickin' spuds,
We're sweatin' every day,

Yet, every time the ploo cam' roond
I had a yaird tae dae.

I let the ploo gan' past, and saw
The tatties skitin' faur,
But something happened then that made
Me feel a guid sicht waur.

The language is authentic Cellardyke Scots, with "skitin'" (shooting out) and the rhyme on "faur" (far) and "waur" (worse). And this former tauttie-howker can testify to the despairing feeling as the tractor comes round and uncovers more potatoes in the "dreel" before you've had time to gather the last lot.

What makes Nellie feel "a guid sicht waur" is the ploughman emptying the "creels" of potatoes with horse and cart shouting, "Come on, Nell, hurry up!" which she takes personally until he tells her he was shouting to his horse. Nell's reflections on the horse in question are reminiscent of Burns and his harvest mouse, in their sympathy for a dumb fellow-creature:

I lookit roond and viewed the horse,
And said intae masel

"Yer jist like me, yer wearit (wearied) lass
Yer long face that can tell.

Yer name's the very same as mine
And tho' ye canna speak,
Twa great big een can say a lot
When trauchled here each week."

Nellie has a twist in the tale for the reader. Having earlier spied a "laddie" sitting on another cart bound for Barnsmuir farm, she reveals:

Tae end my tale there's just one thing
That I'll noo tell ye, folk –
Yon laddie in the cairt? – By jings! –
I'm mairrit tae the 'bloke'!

The man that Nellie married, John Moncrieff Smith, is the subject of another book published by Alison Humphries, his and Nellie's great-niece, entitled Memories of a First World War Sailor. It is a first-hand account describing John's experiences as a sailor in WWI and his internment in an Austrian prisoner-of-war camp in Bohemia.

We said earlier that vernacular Scots poets have always

tended to employ standard English for the more solemn type of subject-matter. Many of Nellie's poems fall into this category, e.g. "Jealousy" –

> *... Oh that ugly word!*
> *Your fangs are sharper than the sword ...*

or "Think Again!" –

> *Are you an atheist –*
> *I wonder why*
> *You think that life is finished*
> *When you die ...*

Typically for one born in the Victorian era, many of the poems have a religious flavour, as in "Tomorrow" –

> *When we find the road so weary,*
> *When we shed that silent tear,*
> *There is ONE who is there to help us,*
> *ONE who said "Be of Good Cheer".*

Heartfelt though these verses no doubt are, it is probably the poems in broad Cellardyke dialect that will most please the reader, and Nellie's late niece Joan Kingscott, Joan's daughter Alison Humphries and Alison's daughter Megan Humphries deserve our gratitude for making them available to a wider public.

2. The Language of Cellardyke

The natives of the East Neuk of Fife have always been proud of their local history and traditions, and not least of their distinctive dialect, which indeed has, or had, local variants in the neighbouring fishing villages. In my first year at the Waid Academy, in 1958–9, I was exposed for the first time to dialect expressions from "furth of" Cellardyke, and I remember being puzzled when a classmate from Pittenweem complained that her shoes were "furdit wi' dirt". It took me a minute to realise that she meant "laggert wi' dirt", the acceptable idiom in Cellardyke.

Our local chronicler, George Gourlay, includes snippets of the local speech in his 1879 book Fisher Life; or, the Memorials of Cellardyke and the Fife Coast; for example, in the exchange between skipper Sandy Wood and his crewman Geordie Anderson on the Father and Son one day shortly after the end of the Napoleonic Wars:

"We'd been better at the Glack", said Geordie Anderson, with an eye at the scanty luck.

"Haud yer tongue, man," retorted his skipper ..., "it was better times before you or the Glack was heard of;" the sea referred to being Dunse Law, bearing over the famous ravine at the "Pease Brig", some four leagues to the eastward of the May ... (p. 58)

"Oh, haud yer tongue!" was a phrase commonly used by the Dykers of old as a mild chastisement, and could still be heard in my boyhood, although the pronunciation would be better rendered as "hud" than the west of Scotland "haud".

At about the same time, many east coast fishermen were sailing to the "whale fishing" in Arctic waters in the summer months, where a successful trip could bring financial rewards to compensate for the hand-to-mouth existence of the rest of the year:

"It just turned oor hand," said the honest goodwife, in all ages the Chancellor of the Exchequer in the fisher home ... (p. 59)

Gourlay gives chapter and verse about local fishing tragedies, and the impact of the drownings on local people is given added weight by his use of the dialect, as for example in his account of the loss of Alexander Watson off the Flora in 1819:

> *"Wha is't; wha's droon'd,"* asks the *unfortunate mother, seeing the dejection and sorrow in every face ... till a landsman rudely unclasps all mystery.* *"Gang awa hame, woman; it's yer ain son!"* (p. 68)

The use of the abbreviated "is't" for "is it" is true to the Cellardyke pronunciation.

In 1978–79 a Dutch linguist, Jacob Hettinga, carried out fieldwork into our local dialect for a master's thesis at the University of Groningen. He summarised his findings in an article entitled "Standard and Dialect in Anstruther and Cellardyke", which was printed in the Scottish Literary Journal Supplement No. 14 in the summer of 1981. Hettinga makes some interesting points, commenting for example that:

> *As a result of the lack of occupational variety, there is no great differentiation as*

regards social class. ... Sociologically most of the local population belong to the working class (WC) and lower middle class (LMC) ... The fishermen like to keep themselves to themselves and are said to speak broader than the rest of the community. "They use more of the old Scotch words."

He concludes that this may have been true in the past, but by now, "the only deciding factor is age. Moreover, many Dykers have settled in Anstruther, so that the two communities are now virtually one."

Much of Hettinga's analysis is very technical and statistical, but a few of his conclusions are worth mentioning. Not surprisingly there are differences between the speech of older and younger informants, but both young and old use a long "cah" (can't) instead of the usual Scots "cannae", and "deh" (don't) rather than "dinnae". In words like "everything", "nothing", "think", there is a tendency to pronounce the "th" as a "h". One informant who denies saying this is recorded saying, "I denk so" (I don't think so).

(Another feature of the dialect not mentioned by Hettinga, but which this writer remembers hearing from people of his father's generation, is the deletion of the initial h in words like "'ospital" [hospital].)

One very perceptive remark of Hettinga's relates to the lack, among older speakers of the dialect, of typically Scottish glottal stops replacing t in words like "better", but instead, a tendency to use a glottal stop before t, c and k in words like "motor", "poverty", "local" and "bakery", resulting in these sounds being unvoiced. This phenomenon can be heard in recordings of local bard "Poetry Peter" Smith reciting his poems, e.g. "The Herring" (from my own experience). It is not of course possible to tell from the spelling of Nellie Watson's poems which of these pronunciations she used herself, but her great-niece Alison Humphries has a recording of Nellie and her sister Mary in conversation in 1985 (see Appendix 4 for a transcript).

Just a few years after Hettinga's fieldwork, in 1982, in Anstruther and Cellardyke, a more user-friendly guide to the local dialect appeared in the shape of Mary Murray's In My Ain Words: An East Neuk Vocabulary, published by the Scottish Fisheries Museum in Anstruther and republished in 2016. Mary Murray was a retired teacher and educationalist and the daughter and granddaughter of fishermen. Her book is divided thematically into sections – The Fishing, Full of Wise Saws and Modern Instances, Special Occasions, Childhood, In the Street, Come Awa' Ben, A Guid Clash, No Sae Weel, The Shakin's o' the Poke, Up the Country, Wha Wis Acht Them? and Bye Names. The penultiumate phrase is perhaps one of the best known of all Cellardyke expressions, regarded as typical of the "postitness" (inquisitiveness) of the local fisherfolk, and meaning "who were they?", literally, "who owned them?"

So interest in the local dialect has continued to the present day, and many "Dykers" persist in using the dialect not just in speech but in modern forms of communication such as emails and texts. The only problem with this is the lack of agreement on how to spell their effusions! Although academics and literary luminaries have laboured to produce a writing system that will do duty for Scots as a whole, an agreed spelling system seems as far away as ever, and controversy still attends the vexed question of whether modern Scots can be considered a language or merely a collection of related dialects.

Harry D. Watson
May 2018

Where you see this symbol next to a poem's title,
further notes on the poem and/or image can be found
in the "Notes on Selected Poems" section.

Memories

and

Reflections

NELLIE WATSON

Dedication

In memory of 'Maw', my loving grandmother, who taught me so much about life.

Acknowledgements

The author wishes to thank her niece, Joan, for editing this book and for the research she did to provide the illustrations.

The Winter Herring ✐

Written in 1949

I woonder what has happened tae
The HERRING in the Firth of Forth?
Long syne the boats cam sailin' there –
Frae ports faur sooth, and wast, and north.

A cheery pictur' they aye made
On bonny, clear and starry nichts,
When ower the watter there ye saw
The Firth filled wi' their twinklin' lichts.

Si-Minnins, Anster, Pittenweem
Had herboors every day gey fu' –
Wi' fishin' boats frae a' the airts –
What's happened tae that "fishin'" noo?

It's Anster herboor I've in mind
As I gan' back throughoot the years,
Sae much wis dune tae pit it richt
And noo the HERRING disappears!

The 'Winter Herrin' was a sicht

That one's no likely tae forget,
And competition was braw keen
For that wee fish jist oot the net.

Thae days saw hunder-barrel-shots
That a' were brocht frae oot the Firth,
And sune the herboor was astir
Wi boats a' scramlin' for a berth.

The piers were fu' o' hustlin' folk,
And rows o' barrels packit ticht
And cutsies flee'n aroond and roond
And salesmen shoutin' a' their micht!

The menfolk toiled for mony an oor,
Their womenfolk kept busy tae –
For Ecky Steenson's horse and cairt –
Gaed rumblin' thro' the streets each day –

Wi' plenty torn nets for a'
(Some screeded richt intae the core!)
He jist wi'd shout their names – and then
Dump doon the nets, richt at their door!

A cheery smile aye on his face

(For ne'er a hoot did Ecky care!)

'Ye'll better get them dune,' shouts he,

'Because the morn I'll bring you mair!'

The Hame Toon was sae busy then

And HERRING often filled oor dish,

But noo there is this awfy change –

What's happened tae that HUMBLE FISH?

A busy day on the West Pier, Anstruther, late 1930s. From left to right: Joe Smith, who came from England to buy the "wulks"; Peter Murray, fisherman, son of "Venus Peter"; "Eck" Scott of "Scott and Stevenson", the Carter and Haulage firm. "Eck" is the "Ecky Steenson" portrayed in this poem.

Jealousy

JEALOUSY! (oh, that ugly word!)
Your fangs are sharper than the sword;
Your eyes are so full of mistrust –
You have to SNEAK – you really must!
Oh fool! Why torture yourself so
With that 'imaginary' foe?

Stamp out this evil, cruel thing,
And give your heart a chance to sing,
Life will take on a different hue –
Your sky will be forever blue –
You'll now see through the eyes of trust,
Proclaim your joy! You really must!

To Peter, or Guid Auld Yesterday✐

*A letter in rhyme written to 'Poetry Peter', Cellardyke, at the
New Year, 1949.*

Dear Peter – here's me greetin' you
For 1949!
And I would like tae write aboot
The days o' Auld Lang Syne!

You'll mebby mind – a wee while back –
A crack we had one day;
I chaffed ye for a verse aboot
The 'Guid Auld Yesterday'.

At first ye smiled – and then ye said,
'I canna promise ye –
Ye see, my een are no sae guid
As what they used tae be.'

I was gey disappointed, but
I tried tae understaund;
And woondered if I'd daur ma'sel
Sit doon and try my haund!

So, if ye see mistakes galore
Oh please, jist pass them by;
I ken I'm jist a novice, but
I thocht I'd have a try.

Well! Here it is – and it's aboot
That 'Happy Yesterday' –
The cheery Gospel Temperance
And the Y.M.C.A.

The singing still rings in my ears –
The hymns that a' were His;
And ane that made a joyful noise
Was made tae gan' like this:-

"Oh for a thousand tongues to sing
My Great Redeemer's Praise!"
'Twas sung wi' sic a herty swing –
We'll mind a' oor days.

The New Year's Social was the nicht
That I aye liked the best;
And ane held in the Forth Street Hall
Staunds oot among the rest.

We 'decked' the hall wi' everygreens –
We liked tae see it braw;
And streamers hung – of every hue –
Across frae wa' tae wa'.

And then, when New Year's nicht cam' roond,
In streamed a mighty throng;
And in the Hall that nicht would be
A guid five-hunder strong.

We aye had Dave as skipper; and
We were his happy 'crew';
And we a' rallied roond him, 'cos
We kent he was TRUE BLUE.

Then – there was oor big well-trained choir
A' there in bright array;
And one jist had tae hear that choir
Tae ken what it cid dae!

That a' the folk enjoyed oor songs
We ken that it is true;
But we a' waited for the time

When Dave would call on you –

Tae gie your 'verse' aboot the things
That maittured tae us a',
And aye the way you 'put it ower'
Was jist withoot a flaw.

Thae happy days aye seem sae near
When memories we share,
But, though it seems like yesterday
It's thirty years and mair!

The 'Workers' Social' was grand tae.
My certy! What a din!
For there were games and fun galore
And awbuddy joined in.

The highlight o' that evening cam'
When you slipped through the back,
And re-appeared as Santa Claus –
Complete wi' beard and sack!

Oh what wi'd we a' gie if we –
Wi' a' oor micht and main –

Could jist unfurl the years, and live
Thae scenes a' ower again?

But in my crack I manna miss
The 'Auld Folks' Social' oot,
For that occasion was a treat
And guid tae talk aboot.

The auld wives, they a' looked sae braw
Dressed in their Sabbath clothes;
Their bannet strings a' ironed oot
And tied up in neat bows.

The menfolk in their dickeys, clean;
Their ties a' straight ana;
And, if I mind aricht, I think
I saw a beard or twa!

A sixpence pie placed on each plate
And 'cookies' there galore –
There were nae fancy cakes those days
Back in the days of yore.

Bress kettles were frae cupboards brocht

And made tae shine like gold
And, wi' a smile we poored the tea –
'Twas joy for young and old.

And, as they drank the cup that cheers
Their chatter was sae bricht;
That they enjoyed themselves we ken –
It was their 'special nicht'!

Wi' duets, recitations, jokes,
Choir pieces, and the rest;
Jist ordinary folk like you and me
A' tried tae dae oor best.

There's lots o' changes been since then –
In faushions tae it's true;
Gone are the bannets and the beards –
There's no nae 'Auld Folk' noo!

I see I've rambled on – and yet
There's lots tae talk aboot;
But – no tae weary ye – I'll stop
And leave the rest o'd oot.

But, when we're thankin' Him above

For blessings day by day,

Let's gie a special word o' thanks

For ane ca'd MEMORY!

Think Again✎

Are you an atheist?

I wonder why?

You think that life is finished

When you die?

Have you a garden

That you tend each year?

And do you never pause to think

Your answer's here?

You dig, and dig, and plant,

But, do you make things grow?

'Tis then you wait for nature's work

To give results, you know.

And do you never stop and look

With wonder at it all?

'Cos if you do

Why then, do you

Deny your God –

And build that WALL?

God gives us (oh so much)

Of beauty all around,

And if we'd only look, we'd see

His miracles abound.

So pause, my friend, please think again,

And search your heart anew,

Because – of all God's miracles,

Isn't his greatest – YOU?

The Tattie Howkin'

Written in 1950

This episode I'm gaun tae tell,
It happened long, long syne,
I think 'twas forty years ago –
While I was in ma prime!

Alice and I were bosom pals
Frae lassies at the schule,
Then, shortly efter that, we tried
The job that made this TALE!

'Twas tattie pickin' we wi'd try
And so to "Caiplie Toll",
We hurried there tae pit oor names
Doon on the "tattie roll"!

Then cam' the day when we set oot
(As pleased as we could be!)
My! – did we ken what was in store
For Alice and for me?

A worset shawl was tied aroond

Oor breest, (that was for need!)
Anither ane was flung across
Oor shoothers and oor heid!

A packsheet apron tied across
Oor front (and no just aince!)
'Twas tied baith at the waist and knees –
The like we've ne'er worn since!

Nae "streamlined" driving in thae days,
We were'na quite sae smairt,
Oor "carriage" was gey primitive –
'Twas jist a horse and cairt!

And oh! The job was awfy hard,
And oh dear me! – the pay!
We ached in every limb and bane
For half-a-croon a day!

The first day by, we landed hame,
And syne we had oor tea;
Then straight intae oor beds we gaed
But next day! Oh dear me!

I felt that I'd been lyin' a' nicht
Intae a bed o' stanes,
I never kent until that morn
I had sae mony banes!

Said I tae Mary, "If ye try
And lift ma richt leg oot –
I'll try and mak' the ither ane
Rise up and follow suit!"

Weel, efter twa-three pechs, I rose
And had my breakfast; then
Set oot along the braes, (gey slow!)
No feelin' grand, I ken!

But I was first, and had tae wait
On Alice coming; so
I stood there (wondering if the job
Was worth the pech!) When, Lo –

Here's Alice running up the Wynd
Ay – at an awfy rate;
A' oot o' breath, she said tae me
"I think I'm kinda late."

"Hoo can ye rin like that?" said I,
"And up a Wynd ana?
I'm shure my banes are a' that stiff
They'll hardly move ava."

Weel, up the "Windmill Road" we trekked,
"A silent pair", I'll say,
Oor cairt was waitin' at the tap
Tae start anither day.

Long Wullie Broon was gaffer, but
There wasna time tae blether;
I'm shure he felt the same as us –
He wasna wauken ether!

There was anither cairt in front –
'Twas gaun tae "Barnsmair",
And I cid see anower that cairt
A laddie sittin' there.

Noo, what that laddie was, I micht
Jist tell ye later on,
But meantime, let's jist say, he was

His mither's braw wee son!

We worked gey hard at pickin' spuds -
We're sweatin' every day,
Yet, every time the ploo cam' roond
I had a yaird tae dae.

I let the ploo gan' past, and saw
The tatties skitin' faur,
But something happened then that made
Me feel a guid sicht waur -

A plooman, wi' a horse and cairt
Cam' roond tae taim oor creels,
And this is what he aye bawled oot
When close upon my heels –

"Come on, Nell, hurry up!" and that
Tae me was hard tae chaw;
Why he had aye tae pick on me
I cidna see ava.

"I canna work nae mair," said I,
"I'm sure I'm dae'n my best,"

And (looking roond) "I'm working jist
As much as a' the rest!"

The plooman looked bewildered like,
And what cam made things worse –
Said he, "I'm speakin' – no tae you –
I'm speakin' tae the HORSE!"

(Embarrassment's a great big word
Which means ye feel gey sma;
And that was hoo I felt that day –
Like fading richt awa!)

I lookit roond and viewed the horse,
And said intae ma'sel
"Yer just like me, yer wearit lass
Yer long face that can tell."

"Yer name's the very same as mine
And tho' ye canna speak,
Twa great big een can say a lot
When trauchled here each week."

"Nell" had the job tae tak' us hame –

A task beyond her strength;
And ae nicht, in the "Smiddy Brae",
She "jist gaed a' her length"!

The driver was the first tae jump –
Long Wullie loupit next,
And then we a' got houstered oot
Till they got puir "Nell" fixed.

And then, aince mair, we crawled anower
And doon Kilrenny Road,
Puir "Nell" cid hardly lift her legs
Tae haul that heavy load.

The schule-bairns help noo wi' this job,
They're motored there and back,
And judging by their waves and smiles
They're no a hard-worked "pack".

Anither thing that's different noo
There's been a rise in pay!
They get near-haund as much an 'oor
As we got for a day!

Tae end my tale there's just one thing

That I'll noo tell ye, folk –

Yon laddie in the cairt? By jings!

I'm marrit tae the bloke!

"Bosom pals frae lassie at the schule"

Pause and Think

I mind my own business!
(Yes, we hear it often said)
And oft it seems
The right and proper thing to do –
But 'tis from God
That we should take our cue.

So, if someone you know
Is in dire need,
Who is too modest
His own cause to plead,
Then pause and think;
For God perhaps
Is working then through you
To help that other live anew.

Thank You God✒

1963

Thank you, God, for our wee Home
From whose door we're loath to roam,
For the little gate that ope'd
Into all we planned and hoped

For the front door, painted green,
O'er whose porch can e'er be seen
Roses blooming, climbing high,
To delight the passer-by.

For the window where we see
Ships that sail far out to sea,
For the ever-changing view,
Humbly, we are thanking YOU.

For the roof, so strong and firm,
Keeping us secure and warm,
For the comforts that we know,
For the friends who come and go.

For the garden all ablaze,

Where we love to sit and gaze –

Drinking in YOUR 'work of art' –

'Cos it's here we're near YOUR heart.

Just a little cottage, where

Love and happiness we share;

From whose door we're loath to roam –

Thank you, God, for our wee Home.

Oor Wee Black Puss! ✎

Written in 1952

Long syne we had a wee Black Cat –
I canna mind his name –
I only mind he played his tricks
On awbuddy at hame!

He was a terror – that was true –
Enjoyed life as his richt;
He'd lie around and sleep a'day
And loup aboot at nicht!

'Twas aye at bedtime he'd get up
And stretch hissel, and gant,
And, 'fore ye said "Jeck Robison",
He'd start wi' his CARRANT!

He'd scoot across the flair, and then
(Wi tail and birse well up!)
Spring up the curtain tae the top –
Like one crack o' a whup!

Ay, I can mind ae nicht when we

We're a' in bed and snug,
A "reeshle" started ben the hoose
And each ane cocked a lug.

At first, it soonded like a moose
Among some tooshie paper;
But, sune we kent that it was Puss
Enjoying anither caper!

Paw sleepit in the kitchen bed,
And frae there cam' a soond;
He struck a match and lit the gas
And had a guid look roond.

Then ben he cam', but by that time
Puss had jumped oot o' sicht;
And here I'll say, "'Twas just the start
O' one long, awfy nicht!"

Mary and I (jist lassies then)
Tried no tae mak' a soond;
We stapped the sheet intae oor mooths
And watched Paw hunt aroond!

We heard him mutterin tae hissel,
Syne gie a wee bit roar! –
"If I cid get a haud o' ye
I'll clash ye oot the door!"

But Puss was ower smairt tae be caught
And keepit oot o' sicht;
So Paw gaed back tae bed again –
Oot gaed the kitchen licht!

Noo, a' was quiet for half-an-oor,
Except for twa-three snores
Acomin' frae the kitchen bed!
Then Lo! across the floors –

Puss bounced and bounced and had sic fun,
Tirrup! Tirrup!! Tirrup!!!
Then, reeshle, reeshle – a' his micht
And waukened a' haunds up!

On gaed the kitchen licht again!
PAW, this time, awfy roosed;
But, by the time he strutted ben
Dear Pussy was well "hoosed".

Intae Paw's hat-box there he crouched,
And, when Paw made a move
Puss birrled roond and roond the box
And blinked at him – by Jove!

But faigs! Paw nabbit him at last,
And, like he said before,
(While Puss me-owed and struggled hard)
He clashed him oot the door!

Then Paw put oot the licht aince mair
And crawled back intae bed;
He shuk his pilly, then lay doon
Tae rest his weary head.

Weel noo, ye'd think 'twi'd be the end
O' Pussy's "horsemanship" –
But, he had ither thochts, and there
He let his vengeance rip!

Along the passage – up the stair!
He'd hae his fun, he wud!
Then, doon the stair – step at a time –

He'd thud, and thud, and thud!

And, what was that? 'Twas Paw again –
On wi' the kitchen licht;
Then, thro' the passage tae the stair –
Oh! Wis there sic a nicht!

By this time Maw was oot o' bed,
And ran ootside her door;
"Oh Wullie, what's that noise?" she cried,
As tae the stair she tore.

And, in the darkness there they stood –
PAW Watson and MAW Broon –
PAW – sic a swell in plaidin' drawers,
MAW – in her white mutch and goon!

And, as they stood confabbin' there
Puss bounced tae his delicht;
Then quietness! and twa great big een
Shone brightly in the nicht!

PAW made one grab, cooch him again,
And then, wi' nae mean stride,

He made tae open the back door
And fling the cat ootside!

But MAW said, "Ey, it's poorin' rain,
The puir beast'll get weet;
I've heard that cats just dinna like
Cauld watter on their feet!

Here look! I'll tell ye what tae dae –
He'll bother ye nae mair;
Jist pit him in that basket in
The closet alow the stair!"

So Paw did what his mither said,
And shut the cat in there;
And then they baith gaed back tae bed
And thocht they'd hear nae mair.

But, did that end oor Pussy's pranks?
Oh no – I'm tellin' you!
His racket sune let us ken that –
Which looder, looder grew.

Jings! In that closet you wi'd thocht

A hunder deevils loupit;
For bottles – tatties – goblet lids,
A' aff the shelf he coupit!

So Paw – his patience noo ebbed oot –
Had lit the gas aince mair;
Athoot a word he made straight for
The closet alow the stair!

He grabbed the cat (by ony bit!),
Flung open the back door!
And heaved him oot wi' a' his micht –
Altho' the rain did pour!

Weel, that was that! So back tae bed
Paw crawled – tae sleep, somehow!
But lo! Afore he snored, we heard
A peetifa' "Me-ow!"

Oot on the windysil Puss sat,
The weend a' oot his tail;
And noo he only had the pith
Tae gie an antrin wail!

Then, when we let him in next morn
(Jist like a drookit rat!)
He sune sat doon afore the fire –
A gey cowed-looking cat!

His plicht fair melted Paw's wee hert –
His sins were a' forgiven;
Paw fussed aroond him – gied him milk –
And set his "engine" whirrin'!

So Puss was happy once again
And curled up tae sleep;
And there he lay the whole day thro –
A wee, roond, furry heap!

Here ends the story o' that nicht,
That I've jist telt tae you;
Don't think it was a "mak-ee-up" –
For every word is true!

Sermons

There's a sermon in the dew-drop
In the rose-bud and the leaf;
It's there in every blade o' grass
It's there in the corn-sheaf.

There's a sermon in each flower –
It is there in every hue;
Do you notice it, I wonder?
'Cos that sermon is for you.

Do you see the rose-bush pretty?
Do you smell its fragrance sweet?
Do you listen to the song-birds?
Do you hear their tweet, tweet, tweet?

If you do, then count your blessings,
'Cos you're fortunate indeed;
There are many who would envy
You these blessings – so take heed.

There are sermons all around us
If we take the time to look;

They're unfolded in the pages

When we read the good 'Old Book'.

Happiness

The birds are chirping in the trees,

The "daffs" are dancing in the breeze,

And we are losing Winter's wheeze

'Cos Spring is here!

There is this 'something' in the air,

(From whence it comes we do not care!)

It's great to feel that it is there

Now Spring is here!

Oh, how the lambs jump for delight,

(And isn't it a bonny sight?)

So let us sing with all our might –

Hail! Spring is here!

Memories o' Maw (Oor Granny)✎

Written in 1949

Long syne we had a Granny, but
We had tae ca' her Maw,
That was because she liked it so,
And was her name frae a'.

Oh she was bonnie! That was true
And dainty on her feet,
And we a' loved her, cos you see
Her naittur was sae sweet.

She had nae enemies ava
And I can never mind
O' seein' her angry – and tae a'
She was forever kind.

But on coorse nichts there on her cheeks
Twa red spots we wi'd see;
And we a' kent the reason for'd –
Oor Wullie on the sea!

"Oor Wullie" was her first-born son –

Wha later was oor Paw –
And looking back – his naittur was
A bit like hers ana.

They baith wi'd tell ye what was richt,
And ne'er tae tell a lee,
They walked the "straight and narrow way"
And never gaed agee.

In 1910, we were a' left
Gey young withoot a Mither
And we jist had tae warsel thro'
And a' help ane anither.

But we had Maw aye at oor back
Tae gie us guid advice,
Altho' I'm shure there wi'd be times
We'd be telt mair than twice!

But we were young then, so it seems
There wi'd be some excuse;
But I was aye the ane wha had
The maist cheek in oor hoose!

I'm shure when I look back, I think
On a' she stood aff me,
For I did tease her oft, I ken,
But she jist winked her e'e.

Her sense o' humour was aye guid,
And she enjoyed a joke,
And when a tale seemed ower faur-fetched
She jist said "What a yoke!"

Each nicht, afore she gaed tae bed
She wi'd come doon the stair,
And see that a' was richt wi' us –
Which showed us she did care.

Noo Mary was the eldest, so
She keepit hoose, ye see;
She scrubbed, and cooked, and washed, and patched
For fether, and us three.

Wullie and Tam were fitba daft –
That didna please oor Maw –
And ower and ower she'd say tae them:
"Drap playin' wi' that kick-ba!"

"Ye'll kick the nebs oot o' yer buits
So bum the thing awa,
Yer fether's no a millionaire
And works hard for ye a'."

Each efternin at half-past twa –
(Ahent a braw scrap-screen)
She'd sit intae her easy chair
And there she'd steek her een.

One day the snores were awfy lood,
And awfy shune begun,
So, near the end o' that half oor
I thocht I'd hae some fun!

I tied a morsel o' a rag
On tae a long, long threed,
And lowered it doon ahent the screen
Till it jist reached her heid.

Then, cautiously I slid it doon
Till it jist scruffed her nose;
And there I let it tickle her

While she enjoyed her doze!

She rubbed her nose – aye, aince or twice
(She thocht it was a flee!)
But when I overdid the trick
She guessed that it was ME!

And "BY MY COUNTRY!" cam her words
Like thunder! "I'll sort ye,
I hiv nae ither grandchild that
Wi'd play this trick on me!"

And, Auntie Maggie sitten there
Was like tae spleet her sides!
And, sune we had Maw lauchen tae
And so cut short her chides!

I mind the time when first I brocht
A LAUD up tae the door;
Her head popped oot the wundae, and –
Afore I could count fower –

I heard her say "Helen, is that you –
D'ye ken it's ten o' clock?"

And I would answer "Aye, it's me" –
And passed it as a joke!

But next day she did lectur' me
And said I was ower young,
And, every time I tried that game –
Again wi'd gan' her tongue!

"I'll tell yer Fether!" she wi'd say
(Jist tryin' tae frichten me!)
But Maw's advice gaed in wan lug
And oot the tither – see?

A bit o' bother, noo I'm shure
She'd think me mony a nicht;
But tho' I liked to tease her so –
I loved her a' my micht!

Why is't we Scots are sae reserved,
And keep it tae oorsels –
When we are fond o' ony ane
There seems nae words tae tell.

We shidna wait until they're gone

Tae "Happy Realms Above",
It's while they're here among us that
We shid show them oor love.

Each Sabbath Maw gaed tae the Kirk
As faithful as cuid be,
And, when I saw her dressed, she was
The bonniest Maw tae me!

I liked a lot o' her quaint ways –
That made her jist OOR MAW –
But what did tickle me, was aye
The way she said "BEATS A'."

And that was when she heard a tale
That caused her merriment,
And mony a yarn we had wi' her
That made her "like tae fent".

She was a grand Maw tae us a' –
Her LOVE was without measure;
And tho' she's gone a long time noo,
Her memory we treasure.

Maw

A Day at a Time

Written in 1963

A day at a time – 'tis a' we get,

But, aye a challenge tae be met,

So, let's dae nothing we'll regret

'Cos aince it's dune –

The hardest pairt is tae forget,

And peace we've nane.

The hasty word – when tempers flair –

Can cause a hurt, sae deep, sae sair,

And, mindin' that, let's a' beware,

'Cos, aince it's said –

The conscience stings, and thochts ensnare,

And tears are shed.

Each day we get, live tae the full

Wi' kindness and guid deeds the rule,

Let nane e'er say that we've been cruel

Tae man or beast,

And let the Auld Book be the tool

We use the maist.

God is Everywhere

Written in 1949

I do not understand, when people say
"There is no God" – when all around, each day
We see the Glory of His love unfurled –
In His creation of this lovely world.
There is so much to live for in this life –
The love of father, mother, husband, wife,
Of friends – of sweethearts, and the joy that comes
When little children come into our homes.
The beauty that the changing seasons bring –
The Summer, Autumn, Winter, and the Spring,
Each season having its allotted task,
And we accept it all, but, do we ask –
"How it is every year, when Spring comes round –
That nature stirs to life within the ground,
And little shoots are pointed to the sky
And humbly on the sun and rain rely?"

"What is the driving force behind it all?"
It is not chance that trees should grow so tall!
In everything we see His loving care –
There is no doubt – that "God is Everywhere".

There is a lesson here for all of us;

That we should try to live – and without fuss –

Each day, just as it comes, and look above

And ponder on the story of His love.

And, if we find it difficult to pray

Let's think on Him in our own humble way;

That would be prayer, in every way, sincere,

And help us daily to live without fear,

If we could do this, and always try

To live for others as the days pass by;

Then, wars and strife on earth would surely cease,

And bring to use a true and lasting Peace.

"It is not chance that trees should grow so tall!"

Life's Worries! ✎

Life's getting you down? But why?
Forget that little person known as "I"
And look around you;
So many ways that you could "GIVE" yourself
So try – will you?

Forget the difficulties in the way
And soon you'll find them melting right away,
Now, on your road!
Just give a helping hand along life's way –
You'll shed YOUR LOAD!

Have Faith ✐

When you're bowed down with your grief,
And it seems there's no relief,
When a voice steals in your ear –
"Time will heal" – you will not hear.

You only see that bolted door,
You feel that life for you is o'er,
But there is One who'll understand
And comfort you, and hold your hand.

He'll gently lead you all the way,
He'll give you strength from day to day,
Strength, then, to think of others too –
Who need your help – thus healing you!

Help Someone Today!✒

A smile could go a long way

So smile to someone today!

For you never know

How far it may go

To brighten someone's day.

A prayer could go a long way

So pray for someone today!

Then just leave it there –

Have faith in your prayer –

Letting God give the answer His way.

A "hand" could go a long way –

Give a "hand" to someone today;

You can make time to spare –

Showing just that you care –

Be that friend in a practical way!

And think on someone today –

That someone who's so far away;

Then do write a line

For the sake of "Lang Syne",

Giving joy to someone that way.

Finicky, Aye! But Did Her Best!

Finicky, finicky – that was Jean
Tae hae a'thing shinin' like a new preen;
While the guid-man jist wandered aroon' and aroon'
And woondered jist whaur he cid pit his feet doon!

"This is getting beyond me!" thocht Jock tae himsel
"I gied her braw carpets, but ne'er cid I tell
That the lass I lo'ed dearly (and still do adore!)
Is noo simply soopin' me oot o' the door!"

One day – when Jean seemed tae be in a guid mood
Jock plucked up the courage tae ask where he stood!
"Noo Jean, when we marrit, ye kept the hame spruce,
But the hame that I made, is noo jist a braw hoose."

In a hurtfu' wee voice, Jean just answered, "Oh, Jock!" –
But the tone o' her words gied her man a big shock,
His arms went aroond her (and while the tears fell)
Jock looked doon the years, then thocht tae himsel–

"Noo, why did I blunder, and hurt ma wee Jean –
Wha keeps a'thing shinin' like a new preen;

I might have got ane that was jist a wee slut
And ne'er a clean shirt tae pit on – and nae wut!"

So noo, here's a gratefu' wee man wha can say
Tae ye menfolk wha's thinkin' in just the same way –
If that's a' the fault yer wife has (she's ower clean!)
"Then coont yersel' lucky – appreciate yer Jean!"

The Nosey-Parker

Written in 1954

I chanced tae meet her – (ye ken her kind!)
Wha her ain business can never mind;
A nosey-parker (as you'll see)
She fired this "broadside" straight at me!
"Yer man's retired noo, I believe,"
(Said in a tone that didna deceive)
"What dis he dae wi' his time a' day?
Oh, I'm jist speerin' (if I may!)"

"Weel, noo, I'll tell ye! – Without fail
He peels the tatties, maks the kail,
He cleans the windows, brings in the coal,
And chops the sticks, (that's pairt his role!)
He dis the washin' (nae bother ava!)
He's learned the irenin' job ana',
Patches his breeks, and darns his socks,
Answers the door when someone knocks."

"He digs the gairden, and plants it tae –
Looks efter ma flooers – keeps weeds at bay,
And, when he's got some time tae spare

He looks around – and says, 'What mair?'"
And as I rambled on, oh hoo
Her een – they bigger, bigger grew!
And, when I paused a wee for breath
She took her chance – and this she saith:

"Oh, I'm fair shocked at a' this tale!
(Yer gien yer man a gey raw deal)
But while he's slavin' hard that way,
Jist what are you dae'n a' the day?"
"Ah there! Yer speerin' something noo –
Tae hoose-wark I have bidden adieu;
I'm a 'Lady of Leisure' it would appear –
Is there onything mair ye wi'd like tae speer?"

Tomorrow ✐

Written in 1954

Tomorrow is just round the corner,
Will it bring us hope and cheer?
For today we are so troubled
With frustrating doubts, and fear.

When we find the road so weary,
When we shed that silent tear,
There is ONE who is there to help us,
ONE who said "Be of good cheer".

If in prayer we seek His solace
We will find His presence near,
And we'll meet all our tomorrows –
Meet them calmly, without fear.

"Tomorrow is just round the corner"

Little Things

It's the little things that matter
As we journey down life's road; –
The friendly smile, the kindly word,
Can ease the heaviest load.

To give a helping hand in need,
(And that without ado;)
Not seeking praise – just giving self,
The "Old Book" tells us to.

To bring a light to some sad eye;
To drive away a tear;
All these may seem just little things,
But – to a sad heart – cheer.

A Wee Word Aboot the "Senior Citizen"

The braes are gettin' steeper
And the hymns in the kirk gaun higher!
And is disna seem sae long ago
Since I sang in the choir.

I sang aye tae ma hert's content,
High notes? -Nae bother then!
But hoo the years have creepit on –
Jist like a thief, ye ken.

But let's forget what the years may dae –
For, if the hert bides young,
And if a sense o' humour's kept –
This way we're helped along.

Senior citizens in Cellardyke, circa 1985. L–R: Margaret Corstorphine (Maggie), Mary Smith (Nellie's sister), Gladys Kingscott (whose son had married Nellie's niece Joan) and Euphemia Corstorphine (Phemie).

Fool!

Written in 1958

Yer "up wi' the Joneses!"
And tae nae one ye hark;
Ye must "go one better" –
Tae be braw – what a lark!

Why can't ye be natural
And jist be yersel –
There's naebudy carin' –
Folk jist say "well, well, well!"

Oh, don't be a fool!
(Is it all so magnetic?)
Because, tae the onlooker,
It's simply pathetic!

So, be genuine, be natural,
A' this nonsense jist quell,
Ye'll be happier, I'm tellin' ye –
If ye jist – be yersel!

Thae Awfy Wynds! ✎

The Wynds! the Wynds! Thae awfy Wynds
Whaur were they a' when I was young?
I only ken they're a' there noo
As if frae nowhere they've a' sprung!

I pech up ane, I pech up twa
And then I staund against the wa',
I wait till the "ticker" behaves a wee better
That seems the thing that's noo the pace-setter.

The calendar says I'm noo ninety-one!
It would like tae tell me ana that I'm done!
But I'm no listening, because, ye see,
It would mak things waur for puir wee ME!

So I plod on – heedless of time
And kid ma'sel I'm still in ma prime!
The aches o' the aged, I try tae ignore –
Faur better than girnin', and being a Bore!!!

The Plodder ✎

On and on and on
The plodder plods;
Against his brilliant brother
He sees big odds.

But does that thought deter him?
Not one bit!
Just makes him more determined
He'll not quit.

There's the story of the tortoise
And the hare;
Those who jump ahead with ease –
Those who DARE.

So, on and on, the plodder
Bravely strives;
And one day (through that courage)
He ARRIVES.

The Birthday Party✐

Written in 1987 for Meg

I'm a happy wee lassie – my age is now three
I'm having a party for all who love me.
We'll wear paper crowns and be happy today -
There'll be such a noise on my Happy Birthday!

There's a wee Bonnie Laddie – I don't know his name –
All that I know – he lives way down the lane.
I call him Price Charming 'cos it sounds very nice
And I think when I know him he'll be beyond price.

Prince Charming! Prince Charming! Oh where are you now?
I know you are hiding, but I'll find you, I vow!
And then to my party I'll bid you to come –
I'll treat you to cream buns and ice creams, YUM YUM!

Little lady! Dear lady! I'm happy to say
I'll come to your party – I'll skate all the way!
I'll tuck into all of the good things you've got
I'm WEE but my TUM TUM can hold a whole lot!

One day I'll come back and again we will meet

'Cos I'm your Prince Charming and you are my Sweet.
You'll come to my Party 'cos it's you I adore
We'll dance and we'll sing because then we'll be four.

I'll buy you a ring with the pennies I've got
I'll empty my piggy-bank – spend the whole lot
'Cos the ring that I'll buy you must be of pure gold
With diamonds all round it for all to behold!

And when I grow big I will marry, marry you
'Cos then I'll be strong and will carry, carry you
To Fairyland, and show you all the wonderful sights.
We'll dance with the fairies all round the bright lights.

I'll make you a garland of roses so fair
For a fairy must have one to wear on her hair.
I think that by then we'll have reached age TEN,
And I'll love you for ever, and ever, AMEN!

"Wee Megan", aged 3

Oh Tae be a Granny ✎

Written to Mary, Nellie's sister, in 1948 when she became a Granny.

It's by request I lift ma pen
Tho' what tae say, I dinna ken –
'Tis for a "fifty-odd" auld "Hen"
That's noo become a GRANNY!

I'll never reach that "blessed state".
(The fairies long syne sealed my fate!)
So, wha am I here to relate
The story o' a GRANNY?

But onyway, I'll try ma best,
Wi' words o' sentiment and jest,
Aboot the "wee chick" in the nest
That's made her a prood GRANNY!

She smiles as she bends ower his cot –
(For is he no her ain wee tot?)
She thanks the Guid Lord for her lot –
Noo she's a happy GRANNY.

She lauchs at a' his baby tricks
As in his cot he goos and kicks,
And later, she'll save him his "licks" –
Wha wadna be a GRANNY!

Noo, Mum and Dad jist hiv tae say
A nicht aff they wi'd like tae hae –
The job as "sitter in" she'll dae –
A joy for ony GRANNY!

On washin' days she'll wheel the pram
And proodly show off her "wee lamb";
Hoo did she dae afore he cam'?
Woonders this happy GRANNY.

He'll stretch his limbs oot every day
And sune be big enough tae play;
And then, one day, she'll hear him say,
"Nannie", his name for GRANNY!

Noo, this wee chap – he's jist a bairn –
A raw recruit, but he'll sune learn
Jist hoo tae work wi' a' his darin'
His tactics on his GRANNY!

Nae doot, at times he'll try tae "soond" her –
(And oft afore him she will "flouder"!)
And, like an expert he'll get roond her –
It's great tae be a GRANNY!

If, in a year or twa frae noo,
She hears a stane come whizzin' thro'
Her windae-pane! With much ado,
"Noo, wha did that?" shouts GRANNY!

And, when she hurries tae the door
(On someone's "bleck" her wrath tae pour!)
A wee voice melts her tae the core –
"I cidna help it, GRANNY!"

Tho' intae mischief wi' his chum
Noo dis she say "I'll tell yer Mum"?
Nae fairs! She says, "Ma douggie, come
And bide aside yer GRANNY!"

Each o' the ither aye sae fond,
Twixt bairn and gran there is a bond
That brings oot joys faur, faur beyond

The dreams o' ony GRANNY!

It is this mystery we ca' LOVE –
This precious thing that comes tae prove
That God is aye there up above –
That's why yer happy, GRANNY!

An Aim in View

Written in 1954

An aim in view is good for you
So do give it a try;
And soon you'll find (to your surprise)
Your morbid thoughts will fly.

Why spend your days in aimless ways?
(With nothing to see ahead;)
Do make the effort, and soon you'll find
A fuller life you'll tread.

To wee David Smith, my Grand-nephew, on his 1st Birthday✎

Oor one year auld – altho' he's wild –
We a' do love him dearly;
But if ye try tae mak' him mild –
He'll jist get wilder, yearly!

My guidness me! He'll need it a'
When oot the street he'll play
Wi' laddies – ay, and lassies tae –
Wha's jist as wild, I'll say!

"A braw wee bairn," says Granny Lil,
"And oh so clever he!"
Says Granny Mary doon the stair –
So, clever, he'll better be!

"A warrior," says Granda Rob,
But comes along and seeks
Tae play wi' him on washin' days –
Dressed in his "barkit" breeks!

His Daddy has jist made a gate

And fixed upon the stair-head;
I hear he's awfy roosed, and shakes
It till his face is red!

His Uncle Johnnie did look in
One day – jist for a crack;
"Hee-Haw," said he, and gave a snort –
The Bleck! he snorted back!

The next thing I expect tae hear,
Is him gaun doon the Wynd
Tae try and seek oot Tawse's shop –
A "pokey-hat" tae find.

Noo Jessie, I would say tae you
"Be prood o' your wee chap";
I hear he's tae be awfy braw
In his new coat and cap!

They a' hae gien their verdict, so
Jist let this Auntie say,
"Hullo, my grand wee laddie, and
A Happy First Birthday!"

Dear Dear!

Written in 1948

So, ye blaw yer ain horn?
My! What a reboond!
And, wha's listenin'? I ask ye –
Jist tak a look roond!

So, ye think that yer clever?
Awa and no blaw!
'Cos the folk that are clever
Ye ne'er hear ava.

They get on wi' their job,
(In the background they draw,)
And what's mair – they're ower busy
Tae find time tae blaw!

The Exile's View of Scotland✐

We may wander around quite a bit –
Mak oor hame in a few different places
But aye in oor hert
There's a wee secret place
For auld Scotland and a' she embraces.

We remember her hills and her glens,
We remember the bluebells to gather,
And aye we can see,
Wi' a tear in oor ee,
Yonder hills a' bloomin' with heather.

Ay, the exile gets hame-seek at times,
And, oh, that can cause you sair trouble –
Tae hear the pipes skirl
And tae see the kilt whirl
Gars ye want tae rin hame at the double.

Comes a day there's a chance tae wend hame
And, oh, hoo it sends the hert burnin' –
Oor step noo is brisk
And oor face a' alicht

"Cos tae hame-land we'll sune be returnin".

Oh, dear Scotland, there's nae place tae beat ye.

We're prood o' the land o' oor birth

And when we're faur awa,

Tae ane and ta a',

Yer the dearest wee spot on this earth.

Yes – the dearest wee spot on this earth!

Some Sentiments

Written in 1953

There's love, and there's laughter, there's sadness and tears,
We've a' learned that as we've gaen doon the years;
But we cid say this ('cos we ken that it's true,)
That God in His mercy will aye see us through.
If we live oot oor lives in the best way we can –
And we lippen tae Him, then we wunna gan 'wrang'.

But that disna mean we're tae hae a long face
As we gan through this world (ay and look at the pace!)
God means us tae lach and oor worries tae halve –
For laughter, we ken, is a guid safety valve,
So let us cheer someone in oor humble way –
And help a' we can, whaur we can, day by day.

Some Mair

Published in Gallery of Verse, April 1960

Let's coont oor blessings one by one,

Brek up the clouds ere they have half begun;

Thanking Him aye for mony happy oors,

We'll find oor path jist strewn wi' bonnie flooers.

Nae room for hate intae oor bosoms find

Throw oot the slichts – the things we thocht unkind

Were mebby blessings that cam in disguise

So we should search oorsels –

If we are to be wise.

Puss! Puss!✐

He was just a stray,
But, on that day
He came to stay.

And, there he sat
Upon my mat –
That pussy cat.

Sometimes he'll roam,
But, aye he'll come
A-wandering home.

On my lap he'll squat –
Just to say that
He's my pussycat!

"On that day he came to stay"

Take Time

Take time to stare
At God's world so fair –
You'll be richer by far if you do.

Take time to explore,
There are treasures in store –
Round each corner you'll find something new.

Forgive

Forgive: The Old Book tells us so – and more;

Not seven times, but seventy times o'er;

But, do you heed?

You can't forgive – because the heart's too sore –

You plead.

Forgive: Because, in doing so,

'Twill help to overcome that bitter blow;

Remember, too,

Your soul will be enriched more than you know,

If you do.

The Sunset✎

Written in 1970

As I sat by my window one evening
Towards the end of a fine day in May,
I gazed on a scene of great beauty –
How I wished it had come there to stay!

The "Great Artist" was busy that evening
With colours so varied, so bright,
And the picture – "a breath-taking sunset" –
Was truly a wonderful sight!

The birds were all chirping and happy –
Their bird-song quite filling the air,
As I sat there I felt so uplifted
I found myself saying a prayer:

"Dear Father, just how do we thank You
For blessings like these to enjoy,
Please don't let us take them for granted,
For that would your purpose destroy."

Soon daylight was changing to twilight,

Little stars peeping in on the scene;

And I sat there till late on that evening

And pondered on all I had seen.

Too True!

Written in 1951

The man to envy is the man
Who envies nobody at all;
He cares not for this world's 'gold' –
He's learned (just like the Saint of old)
To be CONTENT.

He's riches far above all others;
He looks on everyone as brothers;
And should that thought be carried far,
The world would never hear of war –
For man would be – CONTENT.

A Guid Lot o' Fun!✐

Some folk think it's a sheer waste o' time
Jist tae sit doon and start pennin' a rhyme;
But, tak' it frae me – aince ye hiv it begun
Ye'll sure find this oot – it's a guid lot o' fun!

Answering a Question✐

It's often been asked me, "when was the time
That I took a thocht tae start pennin' a rhyme",
And noo, looking back, a' that I hiv tae say
Is that, "a' at aince, it just happened one day!"

Twas a wee laddie's birthday (he was just a year auld)
I got him a card – then I was appalled
At the nonsense I read (for a bairn that age!)
'Twas mair for a grown-up – the words on that page!

If I'd haen ma glesses on looking them through
I widna have bocht it (I'm thinkin' that noo!)
I picked it because it had twa 'Donald Ducks'
And I thocht for a bairn it wud gie'm a few "chucks".

So I looked at his photo – and said to him then –
"That's terrible, David!" – Then I took ma pen
And wrote doon the words that I wanted tae say
(I thocht mebby four lines wid dae me that day!)

I expected ana, tae be sweating a' ower
By the time that my lines had become number four;

But here I was left wi' a lot mair tae say –
So I just carried on, and ma pen had its way!

I ken I'm a novice (I'll mak' that quite clear!)
Don't look for perfection, because it's no here;
I jist scribble on for the love o' the thing
And if, tae ma freends a wee lach I can bring –
Then I'll be contented at pushin' a pen
And writing some sentiments doon noo and then.

Notes on Selected Poems

"The Winter Herring" (p. 27)

Nellie's notes on this poem read: "The 'Winter Herrin' was a busy time in 'Anster' during the winter months of long ago – but now?"

In this piece, Nellie paints a picture of a busy, bustling, jam-packed town and harbour, with boats from every port keen to take their share. A noisy and successful place! The term "hunder-barrel-shots" (the term shot being used to mean "catch" in this instance) gives an indication of the amount of herring on offer.

Everyone was involved in this seasonal "harvest", including wives and children kept busy with "the mending" of torn nets.

"To Peter / Guid Auld Yesterday" (p. 31)

"Guid Auld Yesterday" is a letter written in verse, reminding the recipient about Nellie's request to write a verse about social events. Peter Smith, the fisherman poet of Cellardyke, had yet to respond at that time – so Nellie decides to "have a go"! With her usual humour she reminds Peter of the many good times, before and after the First World War: the dressing up and the fashions, the choral singing and how their community pulled together.

Later on, Peter did respond to Nellie's request. He wrote a poem entitled "Cellardyke Auld Folks Social or Tea" (see Appendix 5). It was republished in 2000 and is the final poem in A Selection of Poems. It runs to 33 verses which include vivid descriptions of dress and fashions in days gone by.

Peter Smith ("Poetry Peter") was the fisherman poet of Cellardyke and Nellie's cousin, once removed. He was descended from a long line of fishermen and was born in George Street, Cellardyke, the youngest of a family of six. Peter Smith was born in 1874, so was aged 75 by the time Nellie wrote this poem.

The Gospel Temperance Society which gets a mention held their annual Social on New Year's night, one of the most important nights in the Scottish social calendar. Nellie also mentions the Anstruther Philharmonic Society, a choral society, was formed in 1892 and still exists.

"To Peter" was originally given the title "Guid Auld Yesterday" in the first edition of this book, with verses 1-5 omitted. The poem has now been restored to its original form and bears its original title.

Image: "Off to 'The Auld Folks' Tea'", uncredited original image from the 1993 edition.

Think Again (p. 38)

Nellie's accompanying note for this poem reads: "Recommended for publication. 1954. May 1992: Published in book Scotland."

The Tattie Howkin' (p. 40)

Another well-loved poem in Nellie's "ain Scot's tongue" is the "The Tattie Howkin'". Based in 1910, best friends Alice and Nellie were aged fourteen and fifteen respectively at this time, and had left school that summer. Their money-making enterprise didn't quite work out as Nellie had expected. It was back-breaking work and there were a few surprises and a shock in store!

Nellie's sister Mary makes a fleeting appearance in this piece; at the time she was "keeping house" because earlier that year their mother had died.

The "Wynd" referred to in this poem is Shore Wynd, a street in Cellardyke. The character Long Wullie Broon is an excellent example of how a characteristic was added to a name to distinguish who it was – in this case long meaning tall – and also reminding us how everyone knew everyone else in the village at that time. The farm that forms the seting for the backbraking work is Barnsmuir Farm, situated on the outskirts of Crail.

Last but by no means least, the final line refers to Nellie's future husband: Nellie and Johnnie married fifteen years later, in 1925.

Image: Nellie (seated) and Alice (standing), c. 1910. A handwritten note from Nellie accompanies the image: "My chum and myself. We made these dresses and were so pleased with our effort that we just had to get our photo taken!"

Thank You God (p. 49)

This poem was written in the same year that Nellie and Johnnie bought their first home in 1963 at Burntisland.

Oor Wee Black Puss! (p. 51)

Nellie again writes these verses in a Dyker's "auld Scot's tongue" and tells this true story with great hilarity. Although the subject is given many a comic twist, Nellie's narrative is also an interesting source of social history. For instance, we learn that Paw (their father, William Watson) slept in the "kitchen" bed. Nowadays it is unthinkable that there would be a bed in the kitchen! The bed in question was presumably a 'truckle' or maybe a 'box bed'. At the time the poem is set, Paw's wife had died; Nellie's grandmother, "Maw" (Mary Brown) would have owned the house at that time and lived upstairs. This poem also shows a little about the relationship between mother and her firstborn son, and the fact that, despite living the harsh life of a fisherman (skipper on the "Violet" and later the "Midlothian"), how Willie had a patient and gentle nature. Willie's grand-daughter and avid scribbler Joan Bett was a wee lassie, "Grandpa Wullie" would visit every day to sharpen her pencils.

The poem features the seafaring term "a' haunds up!", an alternative to the better-known "all hands on deck!".

Memories o' Maw (Oor Granny) (p. 62)

This poem paints a picture of "Maw – oor granny", as Nellie would have said. Her name was Mary Brown, and she was Nellie's father's mother. She lived upstairs in 16 East Forth Street when her son, William Watson, lived there with his wife and four children.

Mary Brown (Maw) and Adam Watson were married in November 1861 in Kilrenny, Fife. Both were born in Cellardyke. Nellie's father, William, was the eldest of their ten children.

Nellie's note accompanying the poem reads: "'What a

yoke!' was a favourite saying o' Maw's, and we often laughed about it."

Image: "Maw"

God is Everywhere (p. 71)

Nellie's note accompanying this poem reads: "In serious mood one day."

Image: Bluebell woods, Forest of Dean, Gloucestershire

Life's Worries! (p. 73)

In this poem Nellie uses the interesting phrase "on your road!", which has a double meaning: It can be used to mean simply "on the way" but "on your road" (with the word "road" emphasised) was the phrase – used often – that meant "get on with it, then!"

Have Faith (p. 74)

Nellie's accompanying note reads: "1964. Written to my pen-pal in England when she lost her husband and could not be consoled."

Help Someone Today! (p. 75)

Originally called 'Ways we can help'. Written in 1980.
Note from Nellie: "This was read at the YMCA social by Jeanie Bett."

Tomorrow (p. 81)

Image: An archway on May Island, Fife.

Thae Awfy Wynds! (p. 86)

Nellie's accompanying note reads: "1986. Written after I had come up the wynds from the Post Office. It was a 'sair fecht'!"

The Plodder (p. 87)

Nellie's note on this poem reads: "Recommended for publication (twice). 1953. November 1991: Published in book called Autumn Gold."

The Birthday Party (p. 88)

Nellie dedicated this poem to "wee Megan on her 3rd Birthday".

Oh Tae be a Granny (p. 91)

This charming piece was written to Nellie's sister Mary, who had become a grannie when Nellie's great nephew, David

Smith, was born.

There is good use of the Nellie's "ain words" in the following poem. In the old tongue "wadna" and "wi'dna" both mean "would not". However, there is also a more subtle meaning and this is demonstrated here. In the fifth verse Nellie uses "wadna" and the meaning is "Yes – who wouldn't want this?" – i.e. it's a good thing. Conversely, "wi'dna" would only be used if the meaning was a somewhat stronger "No – this is not good!"

This first verse was omitted in the first edition but has been restored here.

To wee David Smith, my Grand-nephew, on his 1st Birthday (p. 96)

In her notebook, Nellie introduces this poem thus: "Nellie's first attempt at verses in rhyme, written October 1948." She explains why she was driven to pick up her pen in the poem "Answering a Question" (p. 108).

"Tawse's shop" was a local ice cream parlour and the "Jessie" referred to in the poem is David's mother.

The Exile's View of Scotland (p. 99)

After the First World War, Nellie and her maritime engineer husband, John Moncrieff Smith (Johnnie), moved to South Shields, where Johnnie became skipper of various coal tug boats on the Tyne.

Their next move was to Helensburgh, and although they were glad to be back in Scotland, they remained a long way from their families, given the relative difficulties of travel at that time. The couple remained in Helensburgh throughout the Second World War, Johnnie working at the Blackburn aircraft factory in Dumbarton and Nellie taking a part-time war job at The Norman Service, a renovation and repair shop. Incidentally, she wrote about this too!

Puss! Puss! (p. 103)

Nellie tells us in her note above this poem: "In the blackout during World War Two, a wee black pussy was on our doorstep when we were showing some friends out. And he stayed!" Nellie and Johnnie were living in William street, Helensburgh, during the Second World War.

This small black cat must have reminded Nellie of their childhood pet (and his antics – see "Oor Wee Black Puss!").

Image: Black cat, Kilrenny village, 2017

Forgive (p. 105)

In every life there are some "bitter blows", like those in this poem. Nellie experienced deep loss and heartbreak in her lifetime: in 1910 at just 14 years old she lost her mother; in that era, fathers weren't really expected to get hands-on with childcare, which made it all the harder. Then during the First World War a close male cousin, an army officer, died whilst trying to rescue one of his men who was trapped in the "wire". Then in 1922 Nellie's fiancé died in an explosion on board ship, just before they were due to marry.

Nellie's faith in God's word, along with her own positive spirit and commitment to being a good person, helped her weather such storms.

The Sunset (p. 106)

Nellie's note accompanying this bright little poem reads: "May 1970. Holiday at Buckie. Published in the People's Friend 1973."

A Guid Lot o' Fun! (p. 109)

Nellie enjoyed writing letters and regularly corresponded with friends and family. Even in her eighties she still had many penfriends from her time spent living in South Shields,

Helensburgh, Burntisland, and Buckhaven before returning, in later life, to her native Cellardyke. She sometimes wrote to relatives and friends in comic verse, and we still have some these "letters in rhyme" in her notebook, along with Nellie's transcriptions of their witty replies.

Answering a Question (p. 110)

Over time, Nellie's poetry became more well known and more sought after, to be read out at gathering, meetings, celebrations or just treasured and enjoyed by friends and relatives. She obliged by hand-copying the requested verses, up until the time that many favourites were published in the first edition of her book. This happened to coincide with her 98th birthday!

Nellie was often asked the question of how she started to write, and this poem offers one of the reasons, although there are likely more than one. Being an avid letter writer, and keen to keep in touch with family and friends, maybe she often found herself "pen in hand". No doubt she was inspired by Peter Smith, a poetry writing cousin, but perhaps it was also the need for "her ain tongue" which made her put pen to paper.

The 'wee laddie's birthday' referred to is David's first birthday – see "To wee David Smith, my Grand-nephew, on his 1st Birthday".

Appendix 1:
They Made Their Own Hats!

Resourcefulness, creativity, need being the mother of invention – the folk of the East Neuk were used to improvising and they were good with their hands. The women-folk were always occupied, in any spare time, with knitting, sewing or crochet.

After a war-effort stint in a Gretna munitions factory (see also Appendix 4), Nellie returned to work at the oilskin factory in East Forth Street, Cellardyke in 1918, until her marriage in 1925. By that time, best friend Alice had married Nellie's brother Tom and the couple were living downstairs at 6 Rodger Street.

Alice's older sister Lizzie also worked at the oilskin factory, and it was her income that supported her family in Shore Street, Cellardyke in the difficult times after the First

World War. Lizzie Bett was always a career woman. At the factory she became a seamstress and, later on, a knitwear designer working alongside Chrissie Smith, the niece of Provost William Carstairs.

It was Lizzie and Chrissie who designed and made the first Sea Queen ceremony costumes. On a separate note, Lizzie was a good friend to many, and a quiet confidante. Being well read and interested in many things both within and outside her community, she was often asked to give advice. Lizzie was also our family historian, telling us stories of our resourceful ancestors – and making sure we learnt their names.

Prior to a girls' holiday to Abernethy, Uncle Peter's[1] linen shirts (three of them) were used to make hats for Nellie and her friends. Someone recounted the incident in a snippet on the back of the below photo:

"A hat?" he said. "If you want hats, I've got three shirts I've never worn." They "pinched" [copied] *the shape of an oilskin hat at the factory!*

---

[1] Either Peter Brown who was married to Auntie Maggie, born 3/9/1862, Nellie's father's elder sister, or Peter Smith, Nellie's father's youngest surviving brother, who was born 21/10/1877 and married Anne Morris in June 1901.

L–R Standing: Vina Wood, Chris Dick, Mima Jack; Seated: Nellie Watson, Elsie Jack & May Smith (daughter of Peter Smith & Anne Morris)

Recent interest in the oilskin factory and the links with modern waxed jackets brought a film crew to Cellardyke Harbour in 2018. "Inside the Factory", a BBC documentary about the history of the wax jacket and its origins in oilskin technology, was largely brought about by the 2018 revival of the Sea Queen ceremony, for which the Fisherman's oilskins and Herring Lassies' aprons were recreated by artist and Cellardyke resident Richard Weymss.

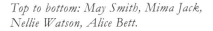

Top to bottom: May Smith, Mima Jack, Nellie Watson, Alice Bett.

Lizzie (Elizabeth Rodger Bett) seated left, with her sisters Annie and Alice. Lizzie, having learnt new skills at the factory, had designed and made their new clothes!

A host of characters from Cellardyke's history, with remembrance of WW1 losses, helped to mark the 70th anniversary of the village's Sea Queen Festival. It was a poignant yet happy and successful occasion, reflecting the enthusiastic community spirit of this very special place. The 2018 Sea Queen was Cellardyke lass, Katie Morris.

Above: The Sea Queen and her attendants pose for a photograph, taken by Lizzie Bett.

Below: Sea Queen ceremony at

Cellardyke Pool in 1948

Above: Provost Carstairs with the Sea Queen, Cellardyke Bathing Pool, 1948

Sea Queen ceremony, Cellardyke Harbour in 2018

Appendix 2:

Cellardyke and the First World War

At the outbreak of war, in early August 1914, the lives of Cellardyke fishermen and their families changed dramatically. With the threat of enemy action, the fishing boats were soon to be requisitioned by the government to be used mostly for patrolling the coastline and for mine sweeping duties. The local fishing crews lost their lively hoods, so many enlisted, and even those owners with boats left at home found that it was hard to get insurance and therefore difficult to "gan tae the fishin".

Peter Smith wrote his poem "The Fisherman", during the First World War and he tells us that the fishermen – the few that were still fishing – were certainly doing their share.

Those, like Peter, who were not deemed fit enough[2] or who were too old, are paying their part in the war to help to provide food.

He reminds us that the dangers were not only for those who enlisted to fight, and fishermen often paid a high price for their catch, even in peace time.

"The Fisherman" by Peter Smith

When Robbie Burns tuned his lyre,
He lifted ploomen life up higher,
Draggit them clean oot o' the mire
Tae' better grund,
Made peer and peasant baith come higher,
And shake a haund.

Oh for a man wi' sic a gift
Tae' clear awa' the sleet and drift,
And gi'e our fisher lads a lift
Sic like as that.

---

[2] Peter Smith's laments not being able to 'join up' in his WW1 poem entitled "This Awfe War", which can be found in *A Selection of Poems* by Peter Smith and was also published in *Memories of a First World War Sailor* by John Moncrieff Smith.

His whar' aboots' I'd try tae' sift,
Syne – raise my hat.

Since sic a chiel' is hard tae' draw
I'll gie' mysel' a wee bit craw,
I dinna mean tae brag or blaw –
It wadna dae.
Jist in a simple word or two
I'll say my say.

Tae you wha maybe dinna' ken
The best o' men – are fishermen,
When I say that I dinna' mean
Their faults are nil,
But, shud ye want ae' proper freen'
Get Him Hissel'.

In times o' peace withoo't a do'ot,
When wars were only read aboot,
Or if we chanced tae get a cloo't
'Twas awfu' little,
The fisher folk were fairly oo't -
No worth a spittle.

We'el dae I ken what I am writin'
Sa'e dinna' think my words are bitin'
My lips I've squeezed til they are whitin'
Wi' perfect scorn.
Tae see the sneerin' and the slightin' –
I'm – fisher born.

But noo when a' thing is at stake,
The fisherman is dae'in' his whake,
I dinna' care a bawbee bake
What nae man says,
For Scotland's, ay! for Britain's sake
Their name we'll praise.

And noo' whar every ocean swells,
Frae Greenland tae the Dardanelles,
They scoor the seas tae save oorsels,
Oor weans and wives.
Ower often there's a list which tells,
The price – their lives.

In khaki class you'll get them tae,
Among the Turks or Flanders grey,
Tae keep the German hordes at bay,

Tho' scarce a unit,
Prood if they're spared tae see the day,
That they were in it.

Weel may Auld Scotland aye be prood,
I ae see the way her sons hae stood,
So that her name be keepit good
Although she sad is,
And name among her hardy crood,
Her fisher laddies.

During this time of war there were many community fundraising initiatives to raise funds e.g. for Red Cross, Belgian refugees or to provide comforts for the troops. In January 1915 a school concert was held by the pupils of Cellardyke Public School which raised £25.8s.6d to send suitable gifts to "Oor Ain Folk in the Navy and Army".

It was from the proceeds of this concert that "a serviceable knife suitably inscribed" was sent to each soldier and sailor from West Anstruther, East Anstruther Cellardyke and Kilrenny. An inscription on each penknife reads: From the Bairns of Cellardyke, Admirers of your Patriotism, February

1915.[3]

This author finds it interesting that the Scottish word for children "bairns" was used when at Cellardyke Public School, at that time, only English was allowed to be spoken and written!

No doubt Nellie, and her best friend Alice, were playing their part in the war effort, as all female children – and some of the boys – learnt to knit.[4]

In mid-February 1915 the *Cellardyke Echo*, the local newspaper at that time, published this short account of knitting for the troops:

> *The women of Cellardyke Parish Church have forwarded to the soldiers and sailors 536 pairs of mittens, 110 pairs of socks, 42 pairs of hose-tops, 36 belts, perseys, 15 shirts, 11 mufflers, 9 knitted jackets, 6 nightshirts, 2 bed jackets, and 2 dozen*

---

[3] Information from Kevin Dunion, personal correspondence.

[4] Children – both boys and girls – were introduced to knitting and hand sewing from an early age. They needed to carry their 'work' out with them when 'going out to play' and the garment, often a sock, was inspected for the necessary increased size on their return home! In adult life, George Keay – a second cousin to Alice – was an accomplished knitter of intricate patterns.

handkerchiefs.[5]

Also noted in local newspapers[6] were meetings where young men, of all trades, were encouraged to do their patriotic duty and volunteer. For those fishermen without work, the pay was an obvious incentive, with extra for those with a wife and family.

Nellie and her siblings, Cellardyke 1914. L–R Mary, Nellie, Bill and Tom – in his Black Watch uniform.

---

[5] Information from research by Richard Weymss.

[6] Coast burgh's *Observer* of 3rd December 1914 gave lists of those men already enlisted; the *East of Fife Record*, on 14th January 1915, published the article "Recruits for Patrol Vessels" with remuneration details.

Nellie was eighteen when war broke out and her younger brother Tom, aged sixteen, soon enlisted in The Black Watch.[7] Alice was seventeen and her only brother John,[8] a fisherman on their father's steam drifter, joined the Royal Naval Reserve.

At this same time, John Moncrieff Smith also joined, serving on the steam drifter 'Craignoon', which recruited others from Anstruther, Crail and Pittenweem. John, would later marry Nellie and be known to us as Uncle Johnnie, survived the war and later wrote of his adventures, and hardships, in 'Memories of a First World War Sailor'. This was first published weekly in 1967 as a six-part newspaper serial[9] and then republished to raise funds for the RNLI, one hundred years after the 'Craignoon', and thirteen other British steam drifters, were sunk in the First World War Battle of

---

[7] Thomas Watson is amongst those listed in local newspaper The Coast Burgh's Observer, 3rd December 1914, as having already been recruited.

[8] John Bett RNR, fisherman of Cellardyke, died in 1915, aged 22. He is buried in Kilrenny Kirkyard and is remembered on Cellardyke War Memorial. For an account of his untimely death see *Memories of a First World War Sailor* by John M. Smith or the leaflet *John Bett RNR, WW1 Fisherman of Cellardyke*.

[9] August & September 1967 in the *East fife Record.*

Otranto.

Meanwhile, the hopes for an early end to the war were dashed and the good folk of the East Neuk of Fife continued to support those fighting. The war dragged on with dreadful consequences,[10] especially for those families who lost loved ones.

Nellie in her munitions fdctory get-up, obviously amused at having her photo taken in such an outfit, despite the grim reality of the amunition stacked behind her.

[10] See *The Democracy of War: Anstruther and Cellardyke in the First World War* by Kevin Dunion

The war brought an urgent need to produce ammunition. Although, at this time, women were barred from serving in military combat roles, they were needed to help out on the 'home front'. Girls from all over Britain were asked to support the war effort.

Nellie and Alice were recruited from Cellardyke and sent to work at Stevenson House, East Riggs, Gretna Green.[11]

This was a residential hostel where they looked after the "munitionettes", the name given to the girls employed in munition (ammunition) factories. The back of their photograph says: "Nellie [Helen Watson] and Ailass [Alice Bett] working as housemaids in the hostel where the munition girls lived. They had made their own outfits."

Many saw helping with the war effort as a way of serving their country but also as a way to gain more independence.

Fishermen's daughters, like Nellie and Alice, were relieved of the drudgery of mending the fishing nets – a task expected of wives and daughters of fishermen. Despite the grim reality of the ammunition stacked in the background, Nellie is obviously feeling amused having her photograph

---

[11] Confirmation received from The Devil's Porridge Museum: 'The photographs were taken by F. S. Gibbs from The Studio Annan'

taken in her utilitarian working clothes.

A family member's account reads: "Sometimes Ailass had to rise at 4 a.m. to make breakfast porridge. Nellie went round with the bell to wake the girls. They scrubbed stairs and floors, did general cleaning and waited at tables. Everyone had to wash up for one hundred girls and the plates were higher than Babs, the scullery maid. At night Babs danced and when they heard Matron coming they jumped into bed with their clothes on!"

In later life the women spoke very little of their time of duty during the First World War. It had been four long and very difficult years for most with the senseless loss of young lives who were often friends or brothers. Nevertheless it was quite an experience for Nellie and Alice, which was never forgotten.

The First World War affected most families in the village with many sad after-effects and one hundred years later, in 2018, a fitting remembrance entitled 'The Quiet Walk' took place in Cellardyke. In silence, villagers walked a route around the streets which remembered those who had lost their lives.

Those who survived the First World War carried on with their lives as best they could. They lived with the dire consequences, which could, and did, last for at least a whole lifetime. My own poem is a tribute to everyone affected, with my own grandfather, Thomas Watson, foremost in my mind.

Home for Christmas – At Last

It's OVER, it's over!
What is?
We can go now
Our duty is done
We can go home
At Last

They carried their scars
Dumb
The friend left behind
The headless corpse
All mud-soaked memories
At Last

Back to the family
Changed
To the old way of life
Unspoken misery
Who understands ...

At Last

No broken bones

Eh?

Well - you were lucky!

No one to talk to

Just in hellish dreams

At Last

Some understood

Gone

The War Memorial

A place to visit

Look at the View

At Last

Those who survived

Aged

And those who died

All did their duty

To give us OUR freedom

At Last

Alison Humphries, November 2018

Cellardyke War Memorial in 2018 (Photo by Meg Kapasi)

Appendix 3:
Nellie's Family History

WATSON – BROWN Family Tree

Information from 'Alison Kigscott Ancestry' by Alexander (Sonny) Corstorphine.

Adam Watson was born in 1836. His parents were **William Watson** (b. 1803) and **Margaret Reid** (b. 1805). Notes for **Adam Watson**: He lived at 16, East Forth Street. He was skipper of the 'Midlothian'. His son William was the skipper of the 'Midlothian' in 1900. His sister Margaret Watson (b. 1837) married James Murray Watson (b. 1834). Notes for Margaret Watson: Known as 'Granny Mags'

Mary Brown was born 1839. (Mary Brown is the **Maw** in Nellie Watson's poem.) Her parents were **John Brown** (b. 1800) and **Mary Hodge** (b. 1799). **Adam Watson**

and **Mary Brown** married in 1861. Children of **Adam Watson** and **Mary Brown** are:

i. **William Watson**, born 17/11/1862 in Cellardyke, Fife.; died 25/11/1936 in Cellardyke, Fife; married (1) Catherine Smith; married (2) Margaret Watson. William was shown as a sailmaker and lived at 13, Rodger Street, Cellardyke in 1891. In 1901, he was shown as a fisherman and lived at 20, Rodger Street. He was skipper of the 'Midlothian' (KY313) in 1900.[12] In 1914, William was skipper/part owner of the steam drifter 'Violet' (KY251).

ii. **Mary Hodge Watson**, born 24/10/1864 in Cellardyke, Fife; married Robert Brown who was born 30/06/1862 in Cellardyke, Fife; died after 1881.

iii. **Margaret Reid Watson**, born 6/10/1866 in Cellardyke, Fife; died after 1901.

iv. **John Brown Watson**, fisherman, born 17/10/1868 in Cellardyke, Fife. In 1900, he was one of the crew of the 'Midlothian'; died 15/12/1908 in Cellardyke, Fife; married

---

[12] See photo in Harry Watson's book *Kilrenny and Cellardyke* p.179

Elspeth Doig; born Abt. 1872 in Cellardyke, Fife.; died 4/5/1963 in Cellardyke, Fife.

v. **Adam Watson**, born 28/11/1870.

vi. **Helen Brown Watson**, born 15/12/1872.

vii. **Henry Watson**, born 20/09/1874.

viii. **Elspeth Watson**, born 17/2/1876.

ix. **Isabella Watson**, born Abt. 1878.

x. **Margaret Murray Watson**, born 21/09/1880.

L: Mary 'Maw' Brown (Mrs Adam Watson) Mid: Adam's sister Isabella 'Granny Bell' Watson (Mrs Charles Marr), R: Adam's sister Margaret 'Granny Mag's' Watson (Mrs James Murray Watson)

SMITH–WATSON Family Tree[13]

The Family of Thomas Smith and Mary Watson.

Thomas Smith's parents were William Smith & Katherine Murray[14] and Mary Watson's parents were William Watson & Margaret Sime.[15]

1. Margaret Smith,[16] born 3/9/1862, married Peter Brown on 4/1/1884

2. Catherine Smith, born 7/12/1863, married William Watson on 7/12/1888

3. Mary Smith, born 3/2/1866, married Alex Cunningham on 14/12/1893

4. William Smith, born 15/12/1867, married Margaret Bruce

---

[13] Copied from Auntie Nellie's copy. The first part taken from the Family Bible (1889).

[14] Copied from Auntie Nellie's copy. The first part taken from the Family Bible (1889).

[15] Margaret Sime was known as Peggy, and she smoked a pipe!

[16] Margaret Smith was known as Auntie Maggie.

on 31/10/1895

5. Lily Ann Smith born 8/11/1869 identical twin, died at one year old

6. Thomasina Smith[17] born 8/11/1869 married John Dick on 20/11/1895

7. Ann Smith born 11/1/1872 married David Dick on 2/1/1900

8. James Smith, born 24/11/1875, married Elizabeth Watson December 1899

9. Peter Smith, born 21/10/1877, married Anne Morris in June 1901

10. John Smith, born 5/9/1879, one year old when his mother died

11. Lilias Scott Smith, born 18/1/1881, one week old when her mother died

---

[17] Thomasina, the other twin, lived to be 87.

Next, their children:

1. **Margaret** & Peter = No children

2. **Catherine** & William = Adam Watson (died aged 4½ years), Mary Watson [married David Smith, ship's engineer = David Smith], Helen Watson [Nellie, married John Moncrieff Smith] Thomas Watson [married Alice Bett = Joan Bett Watson], William Watson [married Cathy, 2nd wife] Note: Catherine (Kate) died in 1910 and William Watson (Skipper of 'Violet') later remarried to Margaret Watson

3. **Mary** & Alex = No children

4. **William** & Margaret = Thomas Smith [killed in WW1 – St Andrew's University – Officer], John Smith [died just after WW1 – influenza epidemic], Willie Smith [married Janet Blyth = 2 boys], Jim Smith [died aged 3 or 4], Peggy Smith [married David McCloud 'Cloudy' = 3 boys: David McCloud, William McCloud, Alec McCloud]

5. (Died in infancy)

6. **Thomasina** & John = David Dick [minister]

7. **Ann** & David = Mary Dick [spinster], John Dick [professor of Engineering married Betty Band = Jennifer Dick, Donald Dick, then remarried Jean = Douglas Dick], Tom Dick [married Jean = David Dick, Alison Dick, Hamish Dick], David Dick [married Helen] = Myra Dick, Anne Dick, then 2nd wife Jean [John's widow]

8. **James** & Elizabeth = James 'Jimmy' Smith [married Jessie Allen = Jenny Smith]

9. **Peter** & Anne = Lizzie Smith (spinster; she helped to look after sweet shop), Annie Brown Smith (married William Band = 2 children], May Smith [married Peter Ramsay = 2 children)

10. (Died in infancy)

11. (Died in infancy)[18]

---

[18] The youngest two children both died within two years of their mother dying (in 1881). The two eldest sisters, Maggie and Kate, were left to look after the house and their siblings.

Circa 1899, L–R Mary, Nellie (with doll) and Tom

Circa 1900. Nellie is with her maternal Grandfather Thomas Smith and her Auntie Maggie Brown. 'Auntie Maggie Brown' is mentioned in 'Memories o' Maw'. It seems likely that the young woman in the photo (Auntie Maggie) is Margaret Smith, Kate's sister. She had no children of her own but, with her sister Kate, had previously helped to bring up the family after their mother died. Maggie was the eldest daughter of Thomas Smith and Mary Watson. She was born in 1862 in Cellardyke, Fife and married Peter Brown, born in 1861.

Circa 1902. L–R: Nellie, Tom, Mary and Bill

Early 1910. L–R: William Watson (father), Helen Watson (Nellie), William Watson (Bill), Mary Watson, Thomas Watson (Tom), Catherine Smith (mother) (Kate).

Circa 1930. A Family Gathering? L–R Tom, Mary, Nellie and Bill

Appendix 4:

Spikin' o' the Auld Times, Lang Syne

Crew of the steam drifter Violet (KY251) L–R: Rob Anderson (married to Mary Watson and who later became skipper of the Violet); Les Brown; Tam Tarvit; Philip Doig; Rob Muir; D. Brown; skipper William Watson (Nellie and Mary's father); Jocky Watson (harbourmaster)); Jimmy (Jock's son, who would later become harbourmaster) and Jocky Jr. (Jocky's other son). (Kindly shared, via Harry Watson, from the private Watson / Anderson family collection.)

With an old cassette tape recorder and my one-year-old daughter, Meg, I went to visit Auntie Nellie.

As luck would have it, Auntie Mary had also called in to see her sister Nellie – whilst out on her afternoon walk. This conversation was recorded four days after Nellie's 90th birthday on 20th August 1985 at 8 Rodger Street, which was Nellie's home at that time.

It is mostly a conversation between Mary and Nellie.

Their speech on this occasion is a mixture of the "Scottish Tongue" and their "school English" (so called because at school the spoken and written word had to be in English.) In an interview on Radio 4 in 2018, linguistics expert Professor Jane Stuart-Smith described how accents are formed in childhood, meaning that if you are listening to a seventy-year-old then you are listening to an accent from at least sixty years ago. On this basis, my cassette tape features the accents of the 1900s.

Mary is Nellie's elder sister. Mention is made of Tom, who was one of their brothers. (He was later to be married, in 1923, to Nellie's best friend Alice, and they became this author's maternal grandparents – Thomas Smith Watson and Alice Pratt Bett). My baby daughter Meg chatters patiently in the background, to the amusement of her great great Aunties!

My recording starts with Nellie asking what they should talk about:

Nellie: What d'you want us tae mind?

Alison: Maybe you could start with where you lived and where you born.

Mary: I was born in number 20 Rodger Street

Nellie: You went to the schale when you were three year

auld, didn't you?[19]

Mary: Yes. Nellie: Eh? Mary: Yes.

Nellie: I've heard you saying you "ran with the bairns".

Mary: Well, eh, so the "Aunties" used to tell me.

Nellie: The "Aunties" telt you.

Mary: Eh, when the bell rang, I just ran with the bairns, and got into the school and the lads telt my Mum, and she says, I kent where you were, and you were quite safe, and the teachers must have just accepted me, see, and I just ran with the rest.

Nellie: I canna mind the first day I went to school. I canna mind o' that.

Mary: I stayed down at number 20 Rodger Street at that time, and I just ran doon – that gate wasn't there and I ran right doon.

---

[19] In the middle of the 19th century, the only school in Cellardyke was the Infant School on the Braehead, at the top of the Urquhart Wynd. This catered for very young children only, probably for those in their first three years at school. Older children, who had not yet reached the school leaving age of twelve, had to make the journey to Kilrenny School, by using the muddy tracks to get there. A new school was built in Cellardyke in 1878 to cater for all ages, but Kilrenny School did not close until about 1936, when there would be less than twenty on its school roll. The new Cellardyke Primary School was still not found to be big enough, therefore it was enlarged in 1896 and served the community well until it was closed in 2003, in favour of a new primary school in Anstruther. (Alexander Corstorphine, 2009, Cellardyke Residents Association Website.)

Nellie: I expect you'll mind mair o'd than I will. Wire in!

[Chatter and laughter]

Cellardyke Public School, circa 1902. Nellie may be front row, fourth from left.

Mary: I can mind o' Miss Rennie, she was headmistress, infant mistress, and she was very good. She taught us singing and, eh, dancing, just the simple dancing, and I remember singing my first solo, I remember being six years old. Four of us stood in a row, and it was the closing day and it was a concert and the parents were there. And oor mother was there, dressed wi' a hat and coat, which was most unusual for a weekday – they were ay sae busy mendin' nets.[20] And that day, four of us were standing in a row. I was Spring, and there was Summer, Autumn, Winter, and we each had a bit to sing. And, eh, I think ma mother was upset wonderin' how I would manage, but I heard her say to somebody as we were a' coming oot, "I neednae have worried, for Mary just lifted her heid and sang". And there was nothing to worry aboot. 'Course, we were all gaed, as oor teachers would hae had us trained on how tae daed, d' you see? So that was my first solo.

Nellie: Do you mind of the Maypole we had?

Mary: Yes.

Nellie: We went roond and roond, and we couldnae get high enough up, and the swings, we went high, as high as we could get, on the swings. I could mind o' Miss Mitchell, our teacher, and the one time I got a "pover". Now you'll no ken what a "pover" is... you could ask your Mum. [Joan] It was for speakin' in class and she said "You Watsons with your long tongues..." But we had awful good teachers. What else would I tell you now? Eh?

---

[20] Referring to mending the fishing nets from the drifters. Nellie's father William Watson was skipper of the Midlothian (KY 313) and later skipper / owner of the steam drifter Violet (KY251)

Circa 1906. A "sampler" made by Nellie at Cellardyke Public School

Alison: What did you do before you went to school in the morning? Did you have to do any jobs at home, or did you have to help when you got home at night?

Mary: No, in the morning it was just a case of you got your breakfast and getting yourself ready for the school.

Alison: What did you have for breakfast, then?

Mary: Well, I think it was porridge sometimes, porridge when we were little.

Nellie: [who was a wee bit deaf] And we got singing and teaching the singing at the school. And I think, in the morning, was there no a prayer?

Mary: Yes. In the morning, the first thing. We collected in the big room in the morning and eh, I mind o' it now, we sang a song called "Juanita".[21]

Nellie: I think you caud it Warnita, but it was a bonnie song, and we learnt a lot of singing and all. But the three R's was what we got, drummed in tae us, the three R's. Mmmm. And at eleven o clock we got ten minutes off, and we all ran home for a jeelie piece. Aye. We just had time, didn't we?

Mary: We just had time. Aye. To get a jeelie piece – and eat it!

Nellie: And then the mothers all got dressed up on the prize days.

Mary: Aye, that was the only time they did that.

Nellie: That was when we'd go to the big room.

---

[21] A Spanish-inspired love ballad composed by Victorian society figure and social reformer Caroline Norton. Published in 1853, it was the first song composed by a woman to achieve massive sales.

Cellardyke Public School, circa 1909. Nellie is in the middle row, fourth from the right.

Alison: What job did your father do?

Mary: Fisherman.

He was a fisherman and there were aye nets to mend. It was for the herring fishing, mostly, and there were a lot of nets to mend, and that house[22] where I am now, you couldn't keep water off the floor, for that's where the net was – on the linoleum.

We both had to learn mending the nets. We were both menders. Mending the nets, you see. We had the needles and your Granda, [Tom] helped when he left school.

---

[22] The family had moved to 16 East Forth Street by that time.

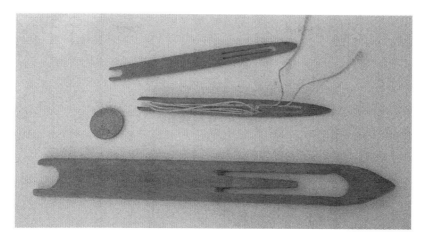

Family heirlooms – needles used for mending the fishing nets, with a 2 pence piece for size comparison.

By that time our mother had died and I was the housekeeper. And I was eighteen.[23] In the summer holidays, Tom [aged 12] helped with the work, and Nellie [aged 15] was at the factory. And, eh, in the morning he would thread the needles for us, for me, and then he would wash the breekfast dishes and then wait at the seaside for a wee while, and then come back and peel the tatties ready for the denner. Tam did that. Then he'd help with the washing up before he went to sail his boat down the seaside. And that was the summertime.

Nellie: And you mind the kail pot was aye on the fire?

---

[23] Mary was born in 1892. Their mother died in 1910.

Mary: Oh aye, we had a big kail pot and a dumpling. "Kail and a dumpling". A dumpling boiled in the kail, in a cloot.

Nellie: You call it broth now, I think, but we ca'd it kail. And the dumpling was good! [Nellie talks to Meg, who is playing with Nellie's washing up bowl.] She's just diverting herself, she's happy an all.

Mary: Tell them aboot the swings. You were aye on the swings...

Nellie: Oh, I couldn't get high enough up on the swings; I was what they ca'd a tomboy! [Laughs] And I mind when they used to bring the nets to dry, we had – I think we had, what did you ca them – we ca'd them galluses[24] [Mary agrees] in the gardens. And we hung the nets on them,[25] and I was aye up as high as I could get. Aye!

---

[24] Regional term for the wooden structures where the fishing nets were hung to dry.

[25] Historical Note: Alexander (Sonny) Corstorphine wote in The Evolution of Cellardyke: "Local legend has it that the name Sillerdykes originated from the fact that the local fishermen hung out their herring nets to dry on boundary walls, and that the fish scales, which were left on the walls, shone like silver. For many years, the fishing community was often referred to with two names, i.e. Sillerdykes or Nether Kilrenny. In later years, the name "Sillerdykes" was anglicised into "Cellardyke", and the name "Nether Kilrenny" lost any preference."

Mary's son David, circa 1930. In the background are several galluses, wooden structures. These were constructed in the back gardens for hanging up the fishing nets to enable them to dry.

Nellie continues: And I was always fond o' horses, aye, and Nana was fond o' coos. Ailass was always there for coos, I mind of that. [Pause] I was always with your Nana.[26]

Nellie: And then we had ... singing, didn't we? We were aye singing, weren't we?

Mary: That's where we got our music and that, a lot of fun. We bought a small harmonium – it cost two pounds, and then we got our music lessons.

Nellie: And we had a dog ca'd Spot and when we started to play the organ[27] Spot got under the chair and howled looder than the organ! [Laughter]

Nellie: But I cannae mind enough o' the school when I was little. It was the last two or three years that I mind, and that was when I met Nana.[28]

---

[26] Ailass (Alice, my Nana) were close friends – "like peas in a pod" – and they went everywhere together.

[27] Another name for harmonium. Popular at this time with three to four octaves of keys, push / pull "stops" to alter the sound and bellows foot pedals.

[28] Nellie and Alice became "bosum pals" and were seldom apart, and from then on the Watson and Bett families were entwined. Both girls left Cellardyke School at the age of fourteen. Nellie went to sew at "the factory" and Alice, whose elder sister Lizzie was already supplementing the family income with similar work, was "needed to help at home". This was a huge blow for Alice, who was bright and loved school.

And that was what we called the sixth standard and the seventh standard. We left at fourteen. We were fourteen years of age when we left the school. And they sort of rolled both of the two top classes, and they put them into one.

The last year we were at school, and I looked roond to see wha was the bonniest lassie, and this was Nana, [Alice] …and I says "would you like to come up and sit beside me?" And she says "yes", and that was the night I went to Shore Street, 11 Shore Street, and we did our lessons sitting on the steps that night, and that was the beginning o' the friendship, and a' you folk comin, efter all that! [Nellie laughs] So…what mair can I tell you?

Alison: What about when you "went to the potatoes"?

Nellie: Ohhhhhh! Oh aye – we'd an awfe sair back! [Laughter] Well, we went in a horse and cairt. It would have been a shire horse.[29] But we really had an awfy grand youth, an awfy grand time when we were little. We were awfy happy, and the fishing used to be "on" January, February, March here, and, you see, the boats all collected here from the north of Scotland, the south

---

[29] See Nellie's poem: "The Tattie Howkin'"

of England, and, oh and it was a lovely sight to see them all at night; the lights were up all over the Firth of Forth.[30]

Nellie: We had plenty of fun. Your Granny Barclay used to say [about Nellie and Alice] "you twa enjoy yourselves". [Nellie then talks to Meg] So, what are you saying "Little Miss" now? Are you tired? Are you going to the beach today? Make sandcastles?

Alison: Oh, you'd better not say that – she'll want to go now!

Nellie: What would you like us to say now?

Alison: What about when you went to help out in WW1. Did you work in the munitions factory in the war?

Nellie: The first war, where the girls lived. That was an experience an' all…!

Alison: Nana worked there as well?

Nellie: Aye, we were both there. Auntie Maggie used to say "we were like twa pearls on a string". We were never separate.

Alison: What was Henry Bett like?[31]

---

[30] See Nellie's poem "The Winter Herring"

[31] Henry Bett was Alice's father, and was owner skipper of *The Alices* (KY 210). To distinguish him correctly he was known as "Ailassies Henry".

Mary: He was an awfe grand man.

Alison: Did he smoke a pipe?

Both: Yes.

Alison: And he had a beard?

Mary: Yes. They struggled after he had his stroke,[32] on his right side; he had trouble trying to use his hands. And when I went along at night he would ask me to fill the pipe.

My recording carried on with happy chatter and laughter, and with Nellie and Mary looking at some of Nellie's poems.[33] Mary then read one of Nellie's longer poems, "The Tattie Howkin'", for us all to enjoy.

Recording time: c. 30 minutes

Alison E. Humphries

---

[32] Henry died in 1943 aged almost 80, having suffered a stroke two years previously. In 1943 there were six of the family living at 11 Shore Street. Henry Bett, his wife Annie Barclay, their eldest daughter Lizzie (who was a knitwear designer) their widowed daughter Alice and her daughter Joan (aged 17) who worked at Anstruther Post Office.

[33] At that time Nellie's poems were mostly unpublished. She copied them by hand for those interested.

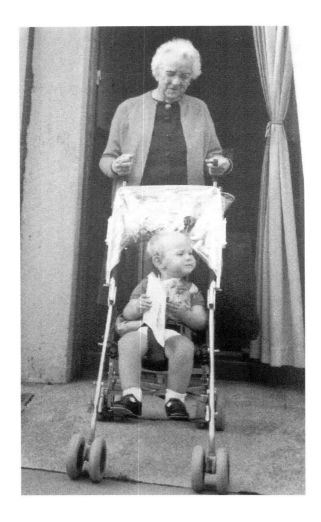

Cellardyke, August 1985. Nellie, aged ninety, enjoying the company of her great, great niece, Meg, aged one.

Appendix 5:
It's Aye the Time tae Dae'd!

(It's Always the Time to Do It!)

Peter Smith, known as Poetry Peter, was sometimes also called the fisherman poet of Cellardyke.

Here he explains that he wants to encourage folk to use their own Scots tongue, to speak it, write it down, and not let it diminish in use.

Peter was consulted by the editors of the Scottish National Dictionary and the compiler of the Linguistic Survey of Scotland, both based at Edinburgh University, about East Fife words and expressions – and the marked differences between the ways people spoke in the various East Neuk villages in those days.

Peter talks of community spirit, and the importance of "keeping the old tongue going", by using those words handed down through the generations in speech or in song. He suggests that if we can keep the old Scots tongue alive then we will be proud of our language, "oor ain tongue", long after others have been forgotten.

"Frae Peter" by Peter Smith

A wee bit screedie wi' the pen
Frae ane o' Scotia's fishermen,
Tae ye wha live in toon or glen,
Cottage or ha':
Auld Scotland's tongue ye mannie len,
Or let it fa'.

When wi' oor cronies we foregather,
Tae hae a crack wi' ane anither,
Words haunded doon frae oor auld mither,
In sang or story,
Aye mak' us feel ilk ane a brither,
Genteel or orra.

Sae dinna let us glutch or gloom,
For fear oor tongue has got its doom,
Losh, if we like it aye will soon
Wi' lofty heid,

When ither tongues that on us froon,

Are long, long deid.

Peter, if he were to "look down" today, would probably be fairly pleased with his "hame toon" and the Dykers who still have a very good sense of their place in the world. The community spirit shown by attendance, interest and support at local events is strong evidence of this. Even if we roam, we still call the East Neuk of Fife "HOME!"

In response to Nellie's request to write about "the Auld Folks Tea", Peter eventually wrote the following poem. It runs to thirty-three verses.

"Cellardyke Auld Folks Social or Tea"
by Peter Smith

I've been at mony an "Auld Folks' Tea",

Tae date my first wad puzzlie me,

I see it whiles thro' memories e'e,

Just like a gleam,

Which vanishes, then a' I see,

Seems like a dream.

But mony ha'e I seen since then,

Auld wives wi' mutches, bearded men,

Wha lookit, aye, as auld again,

As you dae noo;

Toilers by land, or sea, or pen,

We're a' ae oo.[34]

And as they a' sat in their places,

'Twas grand tae see their pleasant faces,

Tho' auld, they'd shamed the Grecian Graces

Nae paint not poother.

They'd flung they things like jocks and aces,

Oot ower their shoother.

We'll tak them first, the ladies fine,

And see hoo they dresst up lang syne,

And, if the young ones dinna mind,

We'll them compare.

Hoo years maks claes and habits dwine,

Syne – disappear.

The Auld sat there, wi' mutch or shawl,

Tae see them noo, wad lookit droll,

---

[34] "We're a' ae oo" = "We're all just pieces of dust".

No paintet up like ony doll,
As we see noo.
Used neither fags nor bogie roll,
Tae gar them spue.

Yon days oor women gaithered whiles,
Tae pairt the mussels doon the Gyles,
Or when the snaw lay on the tiles,
Doon tae the Skaup;
Or gaithered limpits, traivelled miles
Tae fill a caup.

Nae hats or gloves were worn they say,
But only on the Sabbath day,
Then tartan neepyins held the sway
Ower heid or shoother.
Be their hair black, or broon, or gray,
Lass, wife or mither.

Nae kilts wore they, but guid long claes,
It was the fashion – if you please,
Then a' ye saw was jist their taes,
As they gaed by;
Nae lang bare legs on wintry days
As blue's the sky.

But see them dress't up for the Kirk,
Water and soap smoothed oot ilk lirk,
Whiles gied their heids a saucy jerk,
Which cured each wrinkle,
While mony a smile and mony a smirk,
Gard their e'e twinkle.

They mairrit in a braw silk goon,
No only long, but awfie roon,
'Twad made a yacht's sail or balloon,
I've heard them say:
They wore nae hats then, on their croon,
A bannet lay.

Their marriage ring – Australian gold,
Dug by their lads in days o' old,
The young chaps then were jist as bold
As they are noo.
And mony a queer droll yarn they told,
Wad gar ye grue.

We meet them noo, I mean nae herm,
Frae factory, hoose, or kintry farm,
Hair bobbit, shingled, whiles a perm,

Whate'er that be.
They've left nae room noo for a germ,
Hooe'er sae wee.

As for their kilts, when a' things said,
They mind ye o' the Heelant Brigade,
As tae their dinner they parade,
Tho' whiles I greet them.
I'd rather tak the ither side
Whiles, no tae meet them.

But when I tak yon guid auld Book,
And thro' it's pages hae a look,
I read o' lassies there wha took
Sic pride o' dress,
That a' God's precepts they forsook
Wi' sic excess.

They had their cauls and crispin pins,
In nose and lugs there danglit rings,
While roond their cuits an anklit hings,
Or maybe twa;
Then after that, the puir bit things
Jist dwined awa'.

Ower in Isaiah, chap three,

Ye'll see it there, as weel as me,

Hoo bonnie lassies gaed agee

Wi' pride o' dress,

They gaed ower far, as there you'll see,

Losh, sic a mess.

But noo tae lay a' jokes aside,

If we thro' life wad safely glide,

Let's treat God's image aye wi' pride,

But, gang wi' caution,

Satan's warst sin can easily glide,

Intae a fashion.

So noo ye wives and lassies gay,

I class ye a' as wan this day,

Jist for tae let me say my say,

And no omit ye;

Should you be young, or auld and grey,

I'll no forget ye.

Then ere my rhyme on you I drap,

May He, who guides your every stap,

Aye steer ye clear o' a' mishap,

As long's yer here,

And pooer His blessin's in your lap,
Year aifter year.

But yet, ere I lay doon my pen,
I'd say a word aboot the men.
'Twad scarcely be the thing, ye ken,
Tae let them pass;
For as a rule they're whiles as vain
As ony lass.

The men yon days were jist as bad,
The hardy veteran or the lad,
Wha wore a coatie rig was mad,
They got their dues.
Oor women thocht we werena clad
Withoot oor Blues.

When laddies haem frae oor first drave,
Nae doot tae mak us look mair brave,
We thocht we'd venture wi' the lave,
Which tried oor marry,
Tae pay a penny for a shave,
Frae Johnny Harry.

Johnny was a pawky craitur,

Fine he did ken what was the maitter,
As we sled oot and in the gaitter,
Afore his door.
No jist his trade but kindly naitur,
Jist drew us ower.

And syne when he aince got us in,
Some auld droll story he'd begin,
Syne rub the soap a' ower oor chin,
Wi' his saft haund,
While a' he found beside the skin,
Was – a wan man band.

But ither trades were jist the same,
Tae name them ower I ha'ena time,
Wha ca'ed a horse, or mixt up lime,
Were kent thae days
No by the scales, or flooer or grime,
But by their claes.

But see them on the Sabbath day,
Nae Pilot Cloth or Hodden Gray,
They a' dresst in the self same way,
Fisher or Cottar.
Wha' frae the Kirk chose for tae stray

Was ca'd a rotter.

I see them on yon sacred spot,
Their braw tile hat and grand frock coat,
Which cost them mony a hard earned groat,
As back we look.
Splendid they were – compare them not
Wi' Lord or Duke.

And as their characters I scan,
I see that Robbie wasnae wrang,
It's no the garb that maks the man,
It's aye the heirt,
He tells us in yon bonnie sang,
Tae play the pairt.

Yet mony stories still are tauld
O yon lum hats as they grew auld,
As roond the fire when nichts were cauld
We a' did chat,
The bairns throo the flair whiles hauled
The auld lum hat.

Jist this ae story o' the hat,
We guised wi't wi' oor faces black,

Whiles made a bed in't for the cat,
And whiles a marrit.
Then keepit corks in't after that
Up in the garret.

Thae days again can nivver be,
Yet bring the tear draps tae oor e'e,
Reminds us, baith you and me,
That time is short,
We shune maun leave life's tribbled sea
Tae seek a port.

As an auld salt, I say avast,
Some day you'll maybe stand aghast,
While drivin' richt afore the blast,
And I'll say more,
Wi' no an anchor for tae cast,
On yon lea shore.

Then listen while a' thing is bricht,
The Pilot waits on you this nicht,
His fee is paid and a' things richt,
Tak Him the noo.

As longs you keep Him aye in sight

You'll nivver rue.

"Auld wives wi' mutches, bearded men"

Glossary

A

a': all / I

a' oor days: for the rest of our lives

aboot: about

a'body / awbuddy: everybody

abune: above

acomin': coming

ado: fuss

ae: one, as in "ae night" (See also "ane")

aff: off

aft: often, or at the rear

afore: before

agee: off the straight, to one side

ahent: behind

aifter: after

ain: own

aince: once

airt: geographical point, such as direction of wind

alow: below

altho': although

amaist: almost

an': and

ana: as well

ane: one as in "each ane" (See also "ae")

anither: another

anower: inside, within

Anster: the town of Anstruther (pronounced "Enster")

anterin: one "here and there" as in "an anterin ane"

aricht: rightly

a'richt: all right

aroond: around

astir: in a state of movement, anxiety, commotion

a'thing: everything

athoot: without

atween: between

aucht: possession, ownership as in "whas aucht?"

aught: eight

auld: old

auld farrant: old fashioned

auld lang syne: old times, memories of the past

auld Nick: satan

ava: at all

awa: away, "get on with other things", "don't waste your time" or "I don't believe you!" as in "get away"

awfy / awfu'/ awfe / awfie: awful, awfully

ay / aye: always or yes

B

ba': ball

bairn: child

bairns / bairnies: children

baith: both

bake: biscuit

banes: bones

bannet: hat, bonnet

bar: sand formation at the mouth of a river estuary

barkit: everyday clothes

barry: barrow

bate: defeated

bauchle: clumsy

bauld: bald, bold

bawbee: penny

bawbee bake: penny biscuit

ben: inside

ben the hoose: in the other room

bide: stay

bidly ba': wimp

birrled: whirled around

birse: hair, bristle, temper / anger, also hackles

bitin': biting

bittie: piece, part

blaw: blow

bleck: scoundrel

blest: blessed

blether: chat / foolish talk / gossip

bobbit: hair style

bocht: bought

bogie roll: tobacco

bonnie: pretty

boos: bows, the front part of a boat

borry: borrow

bother: trouble, effort, as in "nae bother at a'"

box bed: small double bed – usually four by six foot – and lined with wood at each end forming head board and foot board. Also clad with wood on the side next to the wall with curtains on the open side, it was relatively cosy and warm. In the days when a whole family lived in one room two box beds would be side by side at one end of the room and a truckle bed would pull out from underneath each.

brae: steep slope or road up a hill

brak: break

braw: beautiful, splendid, nice, good looking

breekfast: breakfast

breeks: trousers

breest: breast

brek: break

bress: brass

bricht: bright

brither: brother

brocht: brought

broo: brow

broon: brown

buits: boots

bum: throw away

bumbee: bumble bee

but no': but not

C

ca: call

ca'd: called, call it

ca'ed: made to work

caird: card

cairt: cart

cam: came

canna: can't, cannot

cants: customs

canty: cheerful, full of life

Cardinal Steps: known locally as "the pond", was an open-air swimming pool at the east end of Cellardyke, now partly reclaimed by nature and the sea.

carrant: escapade, hastily organised outing, purely for pleasure

caud: called

cauld: cold

cauldriff: apathetic

caundy: sweets, candy

caunle: candle

caup: wooden bowl

caybin: cabin

Cellardyke: fishing village in the East Neuk of Fife

certy: certainly

cid: could

cidna: couldn't

chaffed: tormented

chap: strike

chap o' nine: nine o'clock chime

chappit: local word for sanctioned

chaw: chew

cheeny: china

chiel: youth, child

chucked: threw

chucks: laughs (a play on words – chuckle: laugh / chucks: chickens)

claes: clothes

clap: place, put

clash: throw (forcefully)

claw: scratch

clime: climate

clocher: phlegm, cough

cloot / cloo't: a cloth or "to slap"

clour: bump or swelling

coatie rig: heavy coat

cocked: raised

codling: small inshore cod

confabbin: talking

cooch: cradled, cuddled, held close

cookies: buns, plain or fruit

cookit: cooked

coont: count

coorse: stormy

coos: cows

coupit: upset, overturned

crack: talk, gossip

creepit: sneaked

croon: crown

cross't: crossed

cryin': shouting

cuid: could

cuist: cast

cuits: ankles

cutsies: seagulls

D

dab: small flat fish, found in sandy water close to shore

dae: do

daed: do it, (as in "how tae daed" – how to do it)

dae'n / dae'in: doing

danglit: dangled

daundered / daunnered: strolled, walked

daur: dare

Dauvit: David

daylicht: daylight

deckit: dressed, decked, decorated

dee: die

delicht: delight

denner: dinner

denty: dainty

de'ils: devils

dicht: wipe

dickeys: best shirts

didna: didn't

dinnae / **dinna**: don't, do not

dings: pleases

dis: does

disna: doesn't

doon: down

doot: doubt

dour: stubborn

draggit: dragged

drap: drop

drappin': dropping

drappit, drapt: dropped, stopped, given up

Drave: name given to the herring fishing season

dreich: miserable, sometimes used when referring to weather

dress't: dressed

droll: funny, amusing

drooned: drowned

drookit: drenched, soaked

dub: puddle

dune: done, finished

dunt: knock, a blow

dwine: wane, decline

dyke: wall

Dykers: people born in the village of Cellardyke

E

East Neuk: the far-eastern corner of Fife which contains the fishing villages of Cellardyke, Anstruther, Crail, Pittenweem and St. Monans

ebbed: gone away

e'e, ee: eye

een: eyes

e'er: ever

efter: after

efternin: afternoon

ere: before

Erin: Ireland

ether: either

ey: exclamation, frequently followed by a rebutting/disagreement, thus strengthening a statement. Also spelled "ay" in some instances

F

fa': fall

fags: cigarettes

fain: gladly

fair: quite, fairly

faigs!: exclamation, "but good gracious!"

faur: far

faushions: fashions

faut: fault

fecht: fight

feck: the greater part, value

feckless: feeble, lacking vitality or worth

fegs!: goodness! really!

fent: faint

fether / faither: father

Fifie: a type of sailing boat popular on the East coast of Scotland during the latter part of the 19th century and into the early 20th century. The Fifie had both a vertical stem and stern and it was said that the very first Fifie was designed and built in a field at the East end of Cellardyke.

finicky: fussy

fit: foot

fitba: football

flair: floor

flee: fly [insect]

flee'n: flying, as in birds flying

fleet: the total number of nets or creels "shot" by a boat

flicht: flight

fling: throw

flooer: flower or flour

flooers: flowers

foreca': forecast

forefaithers: forefathers

fornent: against

fower: four

frae: from

freen, freend: friend

freends: friends

frichten: frighten

fu': full

fule: fool

fund: found

fyke: trouble, fuss

fykie: fussy, someone who makes a fuss, is pernickety

G

gab: dialect, language

gaed: went; or good – see "guid"

gaen: gone

gaither: gather

gaiter: gutter

gairden: garden

gallivant: go on an unnecessary journey, run around idly

galluses: [old local word] wooden structures for drying fishing nets

gan / gang: go

gannet: sea bird, can describe someone who eats a great deal

gansey / garnsey: fisherman's jumper

gant: yawn

gar: make, cause to happen

garb: style of dress

gard: made, caused

garret: attic

gaun: going

gawky: clumsy

gey: very, considerably

gie: give

gied: gave, given

gie'm: give him

gien: given

girnin': grumbling

gled: glad

glesses: glasses

goblet: saucepan

goon: night-gown

gotten: had

gouk: fool

grand / graund: fine / splendid / good

grauvit: scarf

greet: weep, as in "dinnae greet, ma lassie"

groat: crushed grain or oats

grue: shudder

grund: ground

Guernsey: woollen fisherman's jumper

guid: good

guidwill: goodwill

guised: paraded, made a show, way of behaviour

gunnel: rail running around the deck of a ship

Gyles: an area of seashore in Cellardyke

H

ha': hall

hae: have

haen: had

ha'ena: have not

Haikes: a fishing ground near Fife Ness

hale: whole

hame: home

hand-line: a hand-held fishing line, often used on a small boat for catching inshore fish such as small cod

hanker: strong desire as in "Ye needna hanker efter yon!"

haud: hold

haund: hand

haundy: handy

haulyard: halyard, rope

hark: listen

hav'na: have not

heaved: threw, tossed

heelant / heilan': highland

heid: head

herboor: harbour

hert / heirt: heart

herm: harm

herrin: herring

herty: heartfelt

hing: hang

hingin': hanging

hings: hangs

hinna / hivna: haven't

Hirst, the: an area of sea between the May Island and Crail, where the herring gathered to spawn

hissel / hissel': himself

hiv: have

hodden gray: grey coloured material used to make clothing

hoo: how

hooever / hooe'er: however

hoose: house

hoosed: housed

hoose-wark: housework

hotch: jerk, hitch, to bob

hotch potch: a stew or a broth, a mix up; also "hotch potch news", meaning the latest gossip

houstered: gathered together in a confused way

howkin' / houkin': unearth, dig out; also, "Howkin' for loug" (lug worms), the sand worm used as bait.

hullo: hello

hunder: hundred

hustling: busy, fast moving

I

ilk: each

ilka: every

inspek: inspect

in't: in it

intae: into

intermixt: intermixed

irenin': ironing

is't: is it

ither: other

itherwhere: elsewhere

ither: other

itsel': itself

iver: ever

ivery / ivvery: every

J

jaloose: deduce

Jeck: Jack, as in "Jeck Robison" – Jack Robinson

jeelie: (as in "jeelie piece") bread and jam

Jeems: James

jined: joined

jings!: exclamation expressing surprise, as in "goodness!"

jist: just

K

kail: broth soup

keepit: kept

ken: know, as in "a' ken full weel!"

kennin': knowing

kent: knew, known

Kilrenny: A small village, inland from Cellardyke

kimmer: gossip

kin: know; see "ken"

kintry: country

kirk: church

Kirst: Christian, as in my mother's "Auld auntie Kirst"

kist: chest, blanket box, trunk

L

labster: lobster

lachie: cheerful

laddies: boys or young men

lane: lone, alone, solitary – as in "Ye'll meybe need tae gan yer lane"

lang: long

lang syne: long ago

lass: girl or girlfriend

lassies: girls

lach / lauch: laugh

lauchen: laughing

lauchs: laughs

laud: lad, young male sweetheart

lave: remainder, rest

lead: a lead weight, in this context often tied to one end of a hand-line

leal: loyal

lee: lie

leefu': lonely

lees: lies

licht: light

licks: slapping, a smack

limpit: limpet, a small shellfish which clings to rocks

limmer: rascal, rogue, scoundrel, hussy

limminade: lemonade

lippen: depend on

lirk: crease, rumple or fold

load: full

lo'ed: loved

long syne: long ago

lood: loud

looder: louder

lookit: looked

loon: rascal

losh: gosh

loup: leap

loup aboot: jump/leap around

loupin': jumping

loupit: leapt, jumped

loups: jumps

lug: ear

lum: chimney

lum hat: tall hat, straight sided like a chimney

M

ma: my

main: resources, purpose, as in "with might and main", no holding back

mair: more

mairrit: married

maister: master

maist: most

maitter: matter

maittured: mattered

mak: make

mak-ee-up: made up, untrue

manna: mustn't

mare: nightmare

marrit: razorbill

marry: likeness

ma'sel or masel: myself

maun: must

maw: ma, mother (also another local name for herring gull)

May: the Isle of May, a small but historically significant island, and now a wildlife sanctuary, which is situated at the mouth of the Firth of Forth and about five miles out to sea from Cellardyke.

mean: inferior, small

mebby: maybe

mendin': mending "ay sae busy mendin'(fishing) nets"

micht: might, as in: "wi' a' oor micht and main" in "To Peter"

min' / mind: remember

minded: remembered

mire: bog, marsh

mither: mother

mixt: mixed

mixter-maxter: varied mixture, a bit of a muddle

mony: many, as in 'mony an oor' in "The Winter Herring"

moose: mouse

mooth: mouth

morn, the: tomorrow, in the morning

muckle: large, much

munelicht: moonlight

munelicht nicht: moonlit night

mutch: nightcap, women's headdress

mutterin': muttering

ma lane: alone

N

nabbit: nabbed, caught

nae: no, not any

nae fairs!: no fear! / no way! As in "Oh, Tae be a Granny!"

naebuddy: nobody

naittur: nature

nane: none

near-haund: close by

nebs: toes, beaks, bills

neednae / needna: needn't

neepyin: napkin or large handerchief

ne'er: never

neeves: fists

neibors: neighbours, friends

neuk: nook, corner. Also used in place-names of a projecting corner of land, esp. the East Neuk of Fife.

nicht: night

nieve: fist

nivver: never

no / no': not

nocht: nothing

noo: now

O

o': of

o'd / o't: of it

ocht: anything

oft / offen: often

ony: any

onything: anything

onyway: anyway

oo: dust, as in "we're a' ae oo"

oor: our or hour, depending on the context

oorsels: ourselves

oot: out

ootside: outside

opprest: oppressed

ower: over (preposition) or too (adverb) depending on the context

P

packit: packed

packsheet: a coarse cloth

pailace: palace

pairt: part

pally: friendly

parridge: porridge

partan: a type of edible crab

passage: hallway

pawky: shrewd, humorous

pech: puff, pant, wheezy cough, breathe hard from the exertion

peetifa: pitiful

pel-mel: disorderly, confused, rushed, hurriedly, hastily

pennin': writing

pictur': picture

pilly: pillow

pilot cloth: material from which clothing was made

pinch: steal

pinny: apron

pit: put

Pittenweem: a fishing village west of Anstruther, in the East Neuk of Fife

pith: strength, energy

Pittenweem: a fishing village to the West of Anstruther

plaidin': tartan

plicht: plight

Plimsol: Plimsoll Mark, a mark painted on the side of a boat near to the water line to give an indication of how low the vessel is lying when loaded / when empty

ploo: plough

plooman: ploughman

ploos: ploughs

pokey-hat: an ice-cream cone

pooer: power

poored: poured

poorin': pouring, as in "poorin' rain" – very hard rain

poother: powder

pover: [old local word] leather strap / belt, often called a "tawse"

pow: head

pow-wow: discussion

preen: pin

prood: proud

puir: poor

R

racket: unpleasant noise

rale: real

rebound: rebound

redd: ready, prepared, cleaned, put tidy as in "all redd up"

red it oot: cleaned it out

reek: smoke

reeshle: rustle

reuch: rough

richt: right

rife: many, plentiful

rin: run

ring: ring net fishing, a method in which a herring-net would be suspended between two boats which would gradually sail closer to one another with a circular sweep till the net closed and the fish were trapped.

road: way, as in "get on yer road" – 'go on now, on your way"

roastit: roasted

roch: rough

roond: round

roosed: agitated, angry, as in "awfy roosed"

ruch: rough

rumblin': rumbling noisily

S

Sabbath: Sunday

sae: so

saft: soft

sair: sore as in "sair fecht", a struggle, a troublesome task

sale ring: fish market

salt: sailor / fisherman

sanctly: saintly

sancts: saints

sang: song

Santy Clau': Santa Claus, Father Christmas

sark: shirt or vest

scant: small, scanty, scarcity, short supply

scaured: scared

schale / Schule / skule: school

scoor: clean, scour, rub off, or walk at a fast pace

scoot: scurry

Scoot: guillemot

scramblin': scrambling, rushing

scranned: scrounged or feasted, from "scran", an old Scots word for food

scrap-screen: room divider

screeded: torn

screenger: small net used for inshore fishing, scrounger

see'd: see it, saw it

seen't: seen it, saw it

seeven: seven

sel: self

sel't: sold

shate: shoot, cast

Sheilds: South Sheilds, a fishing town in the North East of

England

shingled: hair style for a woman, close cropped

shid: should

shidna: shouldn't

sho'ers: showers, of rain

shoogle / shooglie: to sway, move unsteadily, to rock, wobble, swing

shoothers: shoulders

shot: try, effort, endeavour, also the action of putting nets into the sea, and can also mean the catch, for example "a hunder-barrel-shot"

shu'd: should

shudna: should not

shuk: shook

shune: soon

sune: soon

shure: sure

sic: such

sicht: sight

sillar: money, silver

Si-Minnins: St. Monans, a town in the East Neuk of Fife

sin': since

Skart: cormorant

skaup: scalp, mussel (shellfish)

skellies: rock formations

skilfu': clever, skilful

Skinfast Hyne: Skinfast Haven, the old name for Cellardyke Harbour

skitin: shooting out

sleepit: slept

sleepn': sleeping

slichts: slights, unkind words or deeds

slightin': belittling

slippit: slipped

slutt: a woman with low standards of cleanliness

sma: small

smairt: smart

smiddy: the workshop of a "smith", a blacksmith

snaw: snow

snod: smart

socht: sought

soo: sow

soomin: swimming, as in "Are ye gaun soomin the day?"

soond: sound

sounded: sounded

soopin': sweeping

soopit: swept

speerin': asking

speir / speer: ask, enquire

spent: finished, done, also used to describe a herring who had already spawned and therefore would fetch less money.

spleet: split

spew: vomit, push out

spill: spoil

sprauchle: scramble, clamber, flounder about, flail

sprewl: a fishing lure made from a strip of shiny lead to which un-baited hooks were attached

spruce: spry, smart

spue: billow, surge

spume: spray (apparently derived from Norwegian dialect)

spune: spoon

stampit: stamped, ingrained

stane / **stanes**: stone, stones

stap: step, push, shove

stapped: stuffed, crammed

Star Jeems: James Watson, a well-known Cellardyke fisherman of the early 1800s. As there were many James Watsons in Cellardyke they were more commonly known by the name of their boat. Auld Star Jeems' boat was the *Morning Star*.

staund / staunds: stand, stands

steam drifters: steam powered fishing boats, often 86 feet in length and carrying a fishing crew of eight or nine, including an engineer

steek: shut, close

steerie / steery: astir, commotion, lively, bustling, high spirits, fun

stood: to "put up with" as in "a' she stood aff me"

stoot: stout, can mean healthy, i.e. not frail

stout: stagger, bounce

stowed: stored

straucht: straight

stule: stool

sundered: separated, divided

sune: soon

swell: smart looking person

sweer: reluctant, lazy

syne: then, since, afterwards or ago – depending on context

T

tae: to (preposition) or also, too (adverb) depending on the context

tae'd: to it

tae'm: to him

ta'en: taken

taes: toes

taim / tame: empty

tairts: tarts

tak: take

Tam: Tom

tap: top

tapalsteerie: busy, in a real commotion

tattie: potato / tattered

tatties: potatoes

tauld: told

tawse: leather strap used to punish unruly scholars

teelyer: tailor

tellin': telling

telt: told

teugh: tough

thae: those

the noo: now, just now

the very dab: ideal, just perfect

thegither: together

tho': though

thocht: thought

thraw: oppose, contradict

threed: thread

thro': through

throughoot: throughout

ticht: tight

timmers: timbers

tirrup: commotion, disturbance

tither: other

toon: town

tooshie: rumpled, crumpled up

tow: hemp

towslin': howling

traivelled: travelled

trachle: toil, drag

trauchled: harassed

trews: trousers

tribbled: troubled

tummelt: tumbled

twa: two

'twad: it would

'twi'd: it would

'twas: it was

U

unca: very strange, uncanny

unchancy: dangerous, risky

understaund: understand

unfauld: unfold

W

wa: wall

wad: would

wae: woe

wae's me: woe is me

wadna / **waldna**: wouldn't

wan: one

wantit: wanted

wark: work

warkshop: workshop

warsel: struggle

warst: worst

wasna / **wasnae**: wasn't

watter: water

wattle twigs: twigs, strips of reed

wauchle: shamble

wauken: awake

waukened: woke

waur: worse

weans: small children, little ones (pronounced "wee-ins")

wearit: tired, weary, as in "awfy wearit the noo"

wee: little, small

weel: well

weet: wet

wernae: were not

wha: who

whacket: struck

whake: duty

whan: when

whas: whose

whaur / **whar**: where

whiles: sometimes

whiley: while

whirrin': spinning

whup: whip

wi': with

wi'd: would

wi'dna: wouldn't – spoken more firmly /with stronger emphasis than "wadna"

wi'm: with him

windae: window

windysil: windowsill

winna: will not

wire: knitting needle, also as in "wire in" get going; get on with it!

wis: was

wi't: with it

withoot: without

woonder: wonder

woondered: wondered

worset: worsted

worsit: woollen

wot: to inform

wrang: wrong

wunna: won't

wud: wood, also would, but with more emphasis than "wi'd"

wund: wind (weather)

wut: common sense

wynds: narrow curving roads or pathways, often steep / cobbled

Y

yairs: yards

yaird: yard

yawl: small fishing boat (yawl is the term normally used to describe a vessel under 35 feet in length)

ye: you

ye'll: you will

yer: your, you're

yerkit: jerked, worked

yersel: yourself

yoke: situation, as in "what a yoke"; "what a predicament"

yon: that (one), those over there

yont: beyond

Bibliography

Dunion, Kevin (2007) The Democracy of War: Anstruther and Cellardyke in the First World War. Cellardyke: Kilrenny and Anstruther Burgh Collection. See www.democracyofwar.co.uk

Gourlay, George (1879) Fisher Life or the Memorials of Cellardyke and the Fife Coast. Anstruther: George Gourlay

Murray, Mary (1982) In my Ain Words: An East Neuk Vocabulary. Anstruther: Scottish Fisheries Museum

Ruddick, Sheila (2015) Munitions Workers' Poems. East Riggs: Devil's Porridge Museum

Smith, John M. (2017) Memories of a First World War Sailor. Gloucestershire: Alison Humphries

Smith, Peter Sr. (c. 1951) The Herrin' and Other Poems Anstruther: C. S. Russell & Sons

Smith, Peter (1985) The Lammas Drave and The Winter Herrin': A History of the Herring Fishing from East Fife. Edinburgh: John Donald

Smith, Peter (1998) History of Steam and the East Fife Fishing Fleet. Leven: James K. Corstorphine

Smith, Peter (2000) A Selection of Poems by Peter Smith, the

Fisherman Poet of Cellardyke: Compiled by James K. Corstorphine. Leven: James K Corstorpine

Watson, Harry D. (1986) Kilrenny and Cellardyke, 800 Years of History. Edinburgh: John Donald

Watson, Nellie (1993) Memories and Reflections: An East Neuk Anthology. First Edition. Gloucester: Joan Kingscott

Additional Sources and Suggested Further Reading

"David Beaton: Death"

> https://en.wikipedia.org/wiki/David_Beaton#Death

Corstorphine, A. "The Evolution of Cellardyke"

at https://e-voice.org.uk/cellardyke/cellardyke-history/

Dictionary of the Scots Language: http://www.dsl.ac.uk/

Humphries, A. E. Cellardyke Lassies: Nellie and Ailass in

> WW1 poster, Cellardyke Sea Queen 2018 / The

> Kilrenny and Anstruther Burgh Collection

Humphries, A.E. John Bett RNR, WW1 Fisherman of

> Cellardyke commemorative leaflet, 2015

Humphries, A.E. John Bett RNR, Fisherman of Cellardyke

> poster, Cellardyke Sea Queen 2018 / The Kilrenny

> and Anstruther Burgh Collection

Humphries, A.E. Spikin' o' the Auld Times, Lang Syne.

> Voice recording made in Cellardyke, 1985

Kilrenny and Anstruther Burgh Collection:

> http://www.anstrutherburghcollection.org/

Kingscott, Joan Bett (nee Watson) Family History, notes &

> photographs (private family collection)

Review of Scottish Culture https://www.ed.ac.uk/literatures-

languages-cultures/celtic-scottish-
studies/research/eerc/rosc/volume-eleven

Smith, N. Diary of Two Memorable Holidays (Handwritten,
1950 and 1964; private family collection)

Smith, N. Letters in rhyme between cousin Peggy and me
(Handwritten, 1949 to 1952; private family
collection)

Smith, N. Verses in Rhyme from 1948 to 1987 (Handwritten;
private family collection)

"The true history of the Lochgelly Tawse" (the corporal
punishment belt used in Fife schools during Nellie's
childhood): www.johndick-leathergoods.co.uk/the-
true-history-of-the-lochgelly-tawse-john-johnston-
dick.htm

"The Devil's Porridge Museum":
http://www.devilsporridge.org.uk

"THE GREAT WAR 1914–1918" (timeline)
www.greatwar.co.uk

The Scottish Fisheries Museum, St Ayles, Anstruther
http://www.scotfishmuseum.org/

"Women in WW1"
https://www.theworldwar.org/learn/women

Nellie in later life, enjoying a laugh as per usual

Printed in Great Britain
by Amazon